ACC 936.

920
ROU

194 Rou

196 Rou

D0121557

JEAN-JACQUES ROUSSEAU
and his world

SIR GAVIN DE BEER

JEAN-JACQUES
ROUSSEAU
and his world

THAMES AND HUDSON
LONDON

Frontispiece. Jean-Jacques Rousseau in 1752, when he was entering his most productive period as a writer

Printed in Great Britain by Jarrold and Sons Ltd Norwich

ISBN   0 500 13037 x

PREFACE

It would be hard to find a life more erratic and inconsistent, more tragic but sometimes farcical, than that of Jean-Jacques Rousseau. It would also be difficult to find a set of ideas that have aroused more controversies than his. Lord Acton considered that 'Rousseau has produced more effect with his pen than Aristotle, or Cicero, or Saint Augustine, or Saint Thomas Aquinas, or any other man who ever lived.' These words, from one of the great English historians, command attention even if they do not elicit agreement. They were written before the modern dictators came on the scene, but even they were affected by Rousseau's ideas which still echo round the world. Leaders of former French colonies have turned to Rousseau for guidance. Fidel Castro had a copy of the *Contrat social* in his pocket while fighting in Cuba; later he was to turn to Karl Marx for whom Rousseau was a little bourgeois idealist. Yet it has been held, by Middleton Murry and others, that the Communist Manifesto cannot be fully understood without a grasp of Rousseau's charter of social revolution.

Like him or not, Rousseau is still there, and his life is a curious pilgrim's progress. Without going into the controversies on whether Rousseau inspired romanticism, socialism, anarchism, and communism, I have tried to tell a plain tale within the length of this book. I have written it within a dozen miles of the Lake of Geneva, which supplies the atmosphere for understanding Rousseau's youth, and after spending my own youth in Paris and Versailles, which does the same for Rousseau's later years.

It is a pleasure to express my thanks to Professor Bernard Gagnebin, Monsieur Jean-Daniel Candaux, and Monsieur Charles Wirz, all of Geneva, for information kindly given to me.

Bex
Switzerland

Gavin de Beer

The influence of Rousseau in the French Revolution is seen in this Republican calendar of Year II (1793–4), where the letter 'J' stands for Jean-Jacques Rousseau, shown receiving a bunch of flowers from a child

The Rousseaus were of French origin. In the sixteenth century, Didier Rousseau, of Monthléry, was established in Paris as a wine-merchant and bookseller. He was a Huguenot, and in the days of Henri II and Catherine de Medici this was dangerous for a man uncompromising in matters of faith and freedom. In 1549 Didier emigrated to Geneva where Calvin, only eight years previously, had established his Protestant theocratic state. There, Didier became an innkeeper, married a girl from Savoy, prospered, and founded a family. Of his descendants, David Rousseau, born in 1641, a watchmaker, had fourteen children of whom only three survived infancy, including Isaac, born in 1672, Rousseau's father.

Geneva, seen from the Lake near its southern shore. The Cathédrale St Pierre surmounts the town on its hill, the heart of Calvinist Protestantism. In the background, the Jura Mountains

He was of unstable character, haughty and quick-tempered, and became involved in a fight in the streets with Henry St John, afterwards Viscount Bolingbroke. Isaac's elder sister, Theodora, married an engineer of some distinction, Gabriel Bernard, of an old Geneva family, but within a week of her wedding she gave birth to a child. This was an appalling event in Geneva, but not out of character since Gabriel Bernard's father, Jacques Bernard, Rousseau's maternal grandfather, was constantly in trouble because of his immorality. His eldest child, Suzanne, Rousseau's mother, was born only shortly after Jacques Bernard's own wedding, in 1673. Good-looking, with dark eyes and high spirits, she was once seen,

7

Rousseau's father, Isaac Rousseau, an irascible turbulent man who was obliged to escape from Geneva when Rousseau was ten years old, leaving him practically an orphan to be brought up by his mother's brother Gabriel Bernard and his father's sister Suzanne Rousseau

(*Opposite*) Rousseau's birthplace, 40 Grand' Rue, Geneva, the second house on the left with the arched door

disguised as a man, watching an open-air performance by itinerant players, which earned her a serious reprimand by the clergy. On 2 June 1704, Suzanne Bernard married Isaac Rousseau, and their first child, François, was born on 15 March 1705.

Isaac Rousseau, like his father, was a watchmaker, and the family was passing on the social scale from tradesmen to artisans. But for a time Isaac forsook his workshop because he was fond of music, and became a dancing-teacher. Then, after the birth of François, he left his family and went to Constantinople where he stayed for six years, working as a watchmaker to the harem. He returned to Geneva in 1711 when he learned that his mother-in-law had died. There, at their house in the Grand'Rue, Jean-Jacques Rousseau was born on 28 June 1712, but his mother died from puerperal fever. To this loss many of the aspects of his behaviour in later life can be attributed. The household was then run by Isaac's younger sister, Suzanne. Ten years later, Isaac, who was always ready to abandon his workshop for a day's shooting, trespassed on the land of Captain Pierre Gautier and made matters worse by wounding him with his sword. Proud and egalitarian, Isaac refused to go to prison unless his opponent went there too. As there was no question of this, Isaac escaped to Nyon, in the neighbouring Pays de Vaud. This left Rousseau practically an orphan, and his uncle Gabriel Bernard became his guardian.

Rousseau's heredity on both sides therefore showed a mixture of strong character, tenacity, pride, instability, sensuality and fondness of travel. His brother François ran away to Germany and was never heard of again. Many of the characteristics of his ancestry will be found in Rousseau himself.

For a time, Rousseau was sent to Bossey, a village near Geneva to board with the pastor, M. Lambercier. One day he was accused of breaking a comb, which he had not done, and was soundly beaten by the pastor. This was Rousseau's introduction to injustice. Then, for some other fault, he was beaten by the pastor's sister and enjoyed this introduction to masochism at the hands of Mlle Lambercier. Later, when back in Geneva, he enjoyed more of it from a girl, Mlle Goton, when they were playing together, she at being a school-mistress and he a pupil. These episodes explain other aspects of his attitude towards women.

In 1725 Rousseau was apprenticed, first to a clerk and then for five years to an engraver, Abel Ducommun, a young and brutal man. As a child, Rousseau had been happy and free, but now under his master he became lazy and untruthful, and in bad company he even fell to stealing. He had never been to school and his education was sketchy. While his father was still in Geneva, Rousseau read novels that had belonged to his mother, and then more solid works and classics, including Plutarch and, of course, the Bible. Now he

The village of Bossey, near Geneva, beneath the hill of the Salève, where Rousseau was sent as a child to board with the pastor, M. Lambercier, where he first had experience of injustice

became a voracious reader of books borrowed from a lending library, to the fury of his master who beat him for reading in working time. From his learning, Rousseau had acquired ideas above his station; he felt demoted, resentful of unacceptable authority and started his preparation for war against the world in the cause of freedom.

On Sunday, 14 March 1728, Rousseau went out into the country with some friends. On their return they found the gates of Geneva, which every night were shut at sundown, closed against them. Rousseau decided to put an end to his ill-treatment and ran away. The boundary of the kingdom of Sardinia was so close to that of Geneva that he did not have to go far to reach the village of Confignon, where the priest, Benoît de Pontverre, took him in, delighted at the opportunity of converting a young Calvinist to Catholicism, and gave him a letter of introduction to Mme de Warens, at Annecy.

Mme de Warens exerted the most important influence in Rousseau's life. Françoise-Louise de la Tour was of a noble Protestant

(*Left*) The art of etching and engraving, to learn which Rousseau was apprenticed to Abel Ducommun, a bad master who increased Rousseau's resentment to breaking point

(*Below*) The gate and drawbridge of Rive at Geneva. At sundown on 14 March 1728, Rousseau found it closed on his return from a walk in the country. He deserted Geneva and escaped to Savoy, then part of the kingdom of Sardinia

Françoise-Louise de la Tour, Baronne de Warens, Rousseau's protector, mentor, and ultimately mistress. A convert to the Roman Church, she arranged for Rousseau to abjure the Protestant faith at Turin; on his return she took him into her household for many years

family of Le Châtelard, near Clarens, in the Pays de Vaud. She lost her mother shortly after her own birth in 1699, and was brought up by her aunts at Le Basset, close by. In 1713 she married Sébastien-Isaac de Loys, Baron de Warens, and they settled at Vevey. Headstrong and extravagant, she was always trying to make money. She got into trouble for selling wine in Vevey, of which neither her husband nor she were citizens. Next she started a silk-stocking factory, which soon went bankrupt. Unable to confess her failure to her husband and friends, she decided to run away. On a visit to Aix-les-Bains in Savoy, she had been charmed by the free and easy life lived there, whereas the hard, evangelical climate of the Pays de Vaud repelled her. She therefore determined to go to Savoy.

After collecting together all she could of valuables, plate, linen, furniture and money, she secretly had a boat loaded with them and sailed from Vevey for Évian on 14 July 1726, at two o'clock in the morning. It was a carefully prepared escape, for King Victor Amadeus II was then in Évian, and as he passed on the way to Mass she contrived to throw herself at his feet, begging for protection and a pension. Both were awarded, as she was an important convert and might be expected to effect the conversion of other Swiss heretics, as well as to undertake secret political or diplomatic missions for the King of Sardinia. She abjured the Calvinist religion at the Convent of the Visitation at Annecy. This was the beautiful, charming, cultured, romantic, warm-hearted and ambitious lady to whom Rousseau was recommended by the priest of Confignon.

On Palm Sunday, 21 March 1728, Rousseau met her at the door of the church of Saint-François at Annecy and was immediately captivated by her gracious charm. She read the letter from the Abbé de Pontverre, and told Rousseau to wait for her in her house until after Mass. It was arranged that, three days later, he should set out

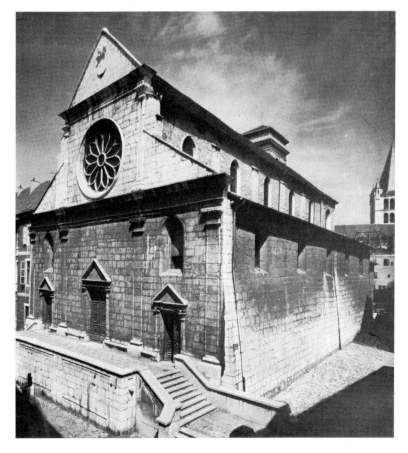

The church of Saint-François at Annecy, at the door of which Rousseau first met Madame de Warens, on Palm Sunday, 21 March 1728, a date indelibly fixed in Rousseau's mind

The Piazza del Duomo, Turin, at the time when Rousseau was there. The street which opens out at the end of the square is the Via Porta Palatino in which is the Ospizio dello Spirito Santo where Rousseau was admitted into the Roman Church

by the Mont-Cenis pass to Turin, where he would be admitted to the Ospizio dello Spirito Santo, to complete his conversion to the Roman Church. He was admitted on 12 April and on 23 April 1728 he was baptized into his new faith with the Christian names of Jean-Joseph. He also had to obtain absolution from the Inquisition for his former heresy as a Protestant. The time spent in the Ospizio served to give Rousseau an idea of the depths to which human nature can descend, shown to him by homosexual 'moors' who became converted in order to beg money for their good deed.

Rousseau then had to make his living. He went into a shop and offered his services as an engraver to the woman who kept it. She gave him some plates to engrave and soon he was helping with accounts and translating letters. Rousseau was smitten with her, but his timidity restrained him from any untoward advances. The woman's husband had been away on a journey; when he returned, a shop-assistant jealous of Rousseau denounced him and he was immediately thrown out. This was another injustice to Rousseau, who again had to find work. After wasting some time, he became footman to Mme de Vercellis and wore her livery. At the inventory held after her death, Rousseau saw a small rose and silver coloured ribbon which took his fancy and he stole it. Its absence was discovered and it was found on him. When challenged he said that another servant, a girl called Marion, had given it to him. It was both a lie and a calumny on his part, and Rousseau never forgave himself for his dishonest and disgraceful action. Both he and Marion were dismissed at once.

Out of work, idle, sleeping in a house where unemployed servants could get shelter for one *sou* a night, Rousseau was in danger of moral disintegration. One day he stood near a well where he knew that girls came to draw water, and exposed himself. He had some difficulty and considerable fright in getting out of this situation. Fortunately for him, he made the acquaintance of a liberal-minded priest, the Abbé Jean-Claude Gaime, who acted as a moral tutor and helped him greatly. Rousseau found other employment, as footman to the Comte de Gouvon, and he also acted as secretary to the latter's son, the Abbé de Gouvon. Although he waited at table, Rousseau wore no livery, and it was noticed that he was already a boy of some erudition. Everything seemed to be going well when Rousseau brought it to an end, because of a sudden impulse to accompany a former fellow apprentice back to Geneva. Rousseau engineered his own dismissal for dereliction of duty, and in June 1729 he set off with his friend.

In reality, Rousseau never had any intention of returning to Geneva, but Annecy was on the way. There he found again the kind and warm-hearted Mme de Warens, who welcomed him and gave him a room in her house. She became 'Maman' to him, and she called him 'Petit'. She had never had a child, he had never known a mother. Attached to Mme de Warens with almost filial piety when she was present, he found that he was even more devoted to her when she was absent, because of a feeling of anxiety for her which gave him pain. He was already living on his imagination.

A profession must be found for him. At about that time fire broke out in a monastery adjoining Mme de Warens's house, and there was danger that the wind would make the flames spread to it. The Bishop of Annecy came, and he, Mme de Warens and Rousseau prayed on their knees in the garden. The wind changed and the house was saved. Rousseau signed a certificate that he was a witness of this miracle. Considering the views that he held later, this fact was remarkable; but at the time it was in harmony with the plan that he should become a priest. He was admitted to the Lazarist seminary at Annecy with a pension from the Bishop and there he made the acquaintance of a liberal-minded priest, the Abbé Jean-Baptiste Gâtier, to whom he became greatly attached. But Gâtier left, and Rousseau found that two months in the seminary was enough for him.

As his passion was for music, he entered the cathedral music school, under Jacques Le Maistre, of whom Rousseau became very

(*Left*) Rousseau's adventure with Mlle de Graffenried and Mlle Galley quickly caught the fancy of Rousseau's admirers. Here a print shows him guiding the young women's horses across a ford and (*right*) the 'idyll of the cherry orchard'. Rousseau on a ladder picks cherries which he throws down to Mlle de Graffenried and Mlle Galley

fond. But in April 1730, Le Maistre quarrelled with the precentor of the cathedral and left. Mme de Warens esteemed him highly, and at her request Rousseau accompanied him to Lyons. There, in the street, Le Maistre had an epileptic fit. Rousseau called for help, made known the name of the inn where the sick man was staying and deserted his friend and companion, then and there. This was another shameful episode with which he reproached himself.

On his return to Annecy, Rousseau found that Mme de Warens had gone to Paris, presumably on one of her secret missions. Left to himself, Rousseau began a period of desultory wandering. He walked to Thônes where he met two girls, Mlle de Graffenried and Mlle Galley, on horseback. As they were having difficulty in getting their horses to ford a stream, Rousseau guided them across. He had inherited his mother's good looks with dark eyes and brown hair, and must have been attractive. The girls made him accompany them and teased him unmercifully. Mlle de Graffenried took him up on her horse behind her and he clasped her round the waist to keep his balance. His heart was beating so hard that she felt it, and told him that hers was also beating hard. He was too timid to raise his clasped hands to the level of her heart. The girls took him to a cherry orchard where he climbed a ladder to pick cherries for them and Mlle Galley, leaning forward, left a gap in her bodice sufficiently

Lausanne where, under the name of Vaussore de Villeneuve, Rousseau pretended to be a composer

large for the cherries to fall into her bosom. This must have been a difficult experience for the grandson of the lecherous Jacques Bernard.

Back at Annecy, Rousseau found that Mme de Warens's maid wanted to return to her home at Fribourg and Rousseau escorted her at her request, in perfect propriety. On the way, at Nyon, Rousseau's father received him coldly because of his apostasy. From Fribourg he went to Lausanne, to feast his eyes again on the view of the beautiful lake. He had the effrontery to pretend that he was an accomplished composer, under the name of Vaussore de Villeneuve. His knowledge of singing was not bad, but he knew nothing of composition. Nevertheless, he composed a piece to be performed in a private house and conducted it himself. The discords were so frightful that the players collapsed with laughter and played all the louder, so that the effect was deafening. The audience were horrified at this cacophony and the episode did not help Rousseau in finding pupils for music lessons; yet he did have a few.

From Lausanne, in August 1730, he went to Vevey, Mme de Warens's old town, and stayed two days at the Hôtel de la Clef. Somewhat later he was at Neuchâtel, still living on music lessons. In April 1731, in an inn at Boudry (birthplace of Jean-Paul Marat), he met a man who claimed to be the Archimandrite Athanasius

The tablet on the Hôtel de la Clef at Vevey, commemorating Rousseau's visit in 1730

Fribourg in Switzerland, which
Rousseau visited with the bogus
Archimandrite Athanasius Paulus,
collecting money for the restoration
of the Holy Sepulchre

Paulus, collecting money, as he pretended, for the restoration of the
Holy Sepulchre. Rousseau attached himself to this man as inter-
preter, as the Archimandrite spoke Italian but no French. Together
they went collecting to Fribourg, Berne and Soleure. This last town
was the seat of the French Ambassador, who exposed the impostor
Archimandrite and had him expelled. To the Ambassador, the
Bishop of Annecy sent a letter of recommendation in favour of
Rousseau, and as the Ambassador's secretary had a friend in Paris,
Colonel Godard, who wanted somebody to look after a young
nephew, Rousseau set out for Paris with more letters of recommendation and a hundred francs.

Paris had been the Mecca of Rousseau's imagination. He expected to find a city even more beautiful and symmetrical than
Turin, with wide streets. Instead, entering Paris by the suburb of
Saint-Marceau (now the quarter surrounding the rue Mouffetard),
he found a labyrinth of narrow, dirty, evil-smelling streets, with
filthy black houses, poverty, peddlers and beggars. This sickening
first impression left its mark on him. He also found that Colonel
Godard was an insufferable, rich old miser, and in August 1731
Rousseau was on the road again, bound for Lyons.

There his money ran out and he was reduced to sleeping in the
open. One day, a man heard him singing and asked if he knew
music and was able to copy it. This invitation not only saved
Rousseau from starvation at the time but also showed him how he
could earn a little money, knowledge that he put to great use later.

Mme de Warens had moved from Annecy to Chambéry and
invited Rousseau to come there. In another attempt to find a profession for him, she got him into the ordnance survey of Savoy,
where he worked solidly eight hours a day, from October to July of
the following year, 1732. But his passion for music tore him away
from his desk and he returned to giving music lessons. Soon he had
a number of young lady pupils from the best families in Chambéry.

The poor in Paris. This was the sort of scene that must have greeted Rousseau on his first visit to Paris, which he entered by the Faubourg Saint-Marceau

This had an unexpected result. In order to protect him from the amorous snares of his young ladies, Mme de Warens made him her lover, or rather, made him share her favours with her factotum, Claude Anet, a peasant from Montreux who had come over to Savoy with her and become converted to Catholicism. When Anet died on 13 March 1734, Rousseau had Mme de Warens for himself. He felt that he was committing incest.

For the next few years, Rousseau devoted himself more voraciously to reading than ever before. Mme de Warens took a house outside Chambéry, Les Charmettes, which thoroughly deserves its name and is still to be seen, in its garden, with the little oratory that she installed at the entrance to her bedroom. For Rousseau it was an idyllic existence, and one of the last periods of calm in his life.

Les Charmettes, Madame de Warens's country house near Chambéry where Rousseau passed the happiest days of his life. He is represented here, reading

According to the laws of Geneva, Rousseau, now twenty-five years old, had come of age. He went incognito to Geneva to claim his inheritance from his mother, as heir presumptive to his brother François of whom nothing had been heard since his disappearance. He was successful and gave the money to Mme de Warens.

In spite of the happy life that he was leading, Rousseau felt that his health was failing and got it into his head that he was suffering from polypus of the heart, a disease then fashionable. The specialist recommended to treat this ailment was Dr Antoine Fizes of Montpellier, who figures in Smollett's works and Laurence Sterne's Letters. Rousseau set off for Montpellier and on the journey he fell in with another traveller, Mme Suzanne-Françoise de Larnage, with whom he was soon dallying. He pretended to be a Jacobite of the name of Dudding, for no discernible reason, but her seduction of him was complete. It always seemed to be the woman who made the advances. In this case, he stated later that he was grateful to Mme de Larnage for the experience of passionate love she gave him before he died.

Rousseau's biographer, Georges May, has drawn attention to a curious feature of Rousseau's sex life. With blonde women, like Mme de Warens, he experienced a sort of spiritual sexual communion; with brunettes like Mme de Larnage, erotic passion. That was why he did not feel that his escapade with Mme de Larnage had made him unfaithful to Mme de Warens, for what he shared with the latter was quite different from what the former had given him, in his imaginative and emotional view.

After a winter at Montpellier, which did him neither good nor harm, Rousseau returned to Les Charmettes, where he found that another factotum had taken his place. Rousseau withdrew to his books. He had already seen his name in print the year before, when the *Mercure de France* for June 1737 published a song set to music by M. Rousseau de Chambéry. He now continued writing on various subjects, in prose, in verse, songs and music, for his self-assurance was firmly established, his pen fluid and his style a model of eloquence. It was at about this time that he wrote a little opera, *Narcisse, ou l'amant de lui-même,* which later had some success. In a book by Le Maître de Claville, *Traité du vrai mérite,* he read, 'From time to time, a privileged soul is born to preserve in the world the idea of what nature once was in all its purity.' Rousseau had no doubt whatever as to who this 'privileged soul' was to be. Although he was later to pretend that it was not so, he was now already burning with the desire of authorship.

Presently he received an invitation from Lyons to act as tutor to the two sons of M. de Mably, *Prévôt-Général* of the province of Lyonnais; he accepted, and started work in May 1740. It was a rise of several rungs in the ladder of Rousseau's cultural contacts, for

a Nion Le 22e Aoust 1740.

Madame

Je n'ay jamais douté de la continuation de vos bontés envers mon fils, vous ne sauriez vous dementir vous avez l'ame trop belle, je ne sauroit trop vous remercier de luy avoir procuré un employ qui le tire de l'inaction, l'etude est fort belle mais quand on la poussée jusques a un certain point & qu'on a pas du bien on doit chercher des occupations qui donne du pain, je croy qu'il se souviendra toute sa vie de ce qu'il vous doit, pour moy Madame je ne puis que vous admirer & faire des voeux continuels au ciel pour votre conservation & votre prosperité j'ay appris depuis quelques jours que mon fils souffloit si cela etoit vray je serois fort affligé car il est impossible qu'une personne ne se ruine en voulant faire des epreuves continuelles de chimie il est vray qu'on trouve des beaux secrets mais il sont plus utilles aux autres qu'a celuy qui a bien brulé du charbon pour les trouver

Letter from Rousseau's father to Madame de Warens, dated 22 August 1740, thanking her for her kindnesses to his son and for her help in finding him remunerative employment as tutor to the sons of Monsieur de Mably. He also refers to Rousseau's illness as a result of an accident while making chemical experiments

M. de Mably had two famous brothers: the Abbé de Mably, economist and writer, and Condillac the philosopher. Both were to figure in Rousseau's life.

In his new post, the self-taught young man was now teaching other boys and he systematized his work in his *Projet pour l'éducation de M. de Sainte-Marie*, a scheme for the education of the elder son of M. de Mably. His stay in this post was the longest uninterrupted employment that he had undertaken, for it lasted one whole year, but his appointment was not renewed and he returned to Chambéry.

Mme de Warens's affairs were in a very bad state. Her grandiose business plans had gone awry, her pension from the King of

Chanson Negre +

+ j. j. Rousseau
a fait un air
avec la basse pour
cette chanson et d'ipis
La note à la marge
de sa main suivant
la manière de
noter qui es de
son invention.

Lisette quittés la pleine
moi perdi bonheur à moi,
yeux à moi semble fontaine
d'ipis moi pas miré toi.
Le jour quand moi coupé canne
moi songés à Zamour moy
La nuit quand moi dans Cabanne
dans dormir moi quimbe toi.

Sol 3 || 1 2. / 3 / 2 7 / 6. 5 |
      1 5. / 1 3 2 / 1 7. |
1 2. / 3 / 1 6 2 / 1 |
6 5. / 1 / 3 5 / 1. |
3 4. / 5 / 2 3 1 / 2. 3 1 |
7 6. / 3 / 4 1 3 / 5. 1 |
3 4. / 5 / 4 3 1 / 2 |
1 6. / 3 / 2 1 3 / 5   D.C

Rousseau's passion was music, and his pride was the method of musical notation which he invented using figures to denote tones without staves or notes. This is the air which he put to this song, written in his method of notation

Sardinia remained unpaid. Rousseau wrote several business letters for her, in masterly style, and then he fell ill.

During and after his convalescence, Rousseau worked at a system of musical notation that he had invented. Instead of oval-shaped notes on different lines of two staves, with many complicated signs, he used numbers to denote tones, dots above or below them to indicate higher or lower octaves, other signs for sharps and flats, bars to mark the time, all on a single line. Eight lines were sufficient for him to write the whole minuet in Rameau's *Dardanus*. Rousseau claimed that, with his system, it was much easier to transpose tunes from one key to another, and much easier for beginners to learn. He neglected the fact that he was interested in melody, not in harmony.

Armed with his system, his manuscripts and recommendations from his friends in Lyons to leading men in Paris – for example, the great Fontenelle, the Comte de Caylus and even the Duc de Richelieu – Rousseau set off in August 1742 and stayed at the Hôtel Saint-Quentin, rue des Cordiers, near the Sorbonne. Wretched street, wretched hotel, wretched room, he thought, but he comforted himself with the knowledge that many great men, like M. de Mably and Condillac, had stayed there. He soon made the acquaintance of two men who were to count greatly in his life: Daniel Roguin, of Yverdon, a lifelong friend, and Denis Diderot, eventually a lifelong enemy.

On 22 August 1742, the great Réaumur himself introduced Rousseau at a meeting of the Académie royale des sciences; and reading a paper on his system of musical notation was an opportunity for Rousseau to make himself known to the greatest men of science in France. The Académie appointed referees to report on Rousseau's contribution, and they praised the clarity of Rousseau's exposition of his method. They allowed that it might be helpful to singers, but very difficult for instrumentalists and orchestras. They added that the Académie never gave its approval of a contribution unless it was both new and useful. It was not the latter, for the reasons given; nor was it new, for Father Souhaitti had put forward a similar method of notation sixty-five years before.

Rousseau was deeply disappointed and also resentful of what he considered to be the ignorance of the referees, some of whom, in fact, were good musicians. Rousseau decided to appeal to the public over the heads of the Académie, and retired to his hotel attic to write *Dissertation sur la musique moderne*. He also performed an experiment: in three months he taught a young American girl, Mlle des Roulins, who knew no music at all, to read at sight and to sing any air by means of his notation. There was a little controversy over his book, but it soon fizzled out and nobody paid any more attention to his system of musical notation.

Avid for recognition, Rousseau turned to another subject, how to make a flying machine. 'What privilege can birds have to exclude us from their medium, when fishes admit us to theirs?' *Le nouveau Dédale,* however, remained in manuscript.

In 1743 his *Dissertation sur la musique moderne* had an unexpected effect, for it drew him to the attention of Mme Dupin, one of the richest and most beautiful women in Paris, wife of a *fermier-général.* She received him *en déshabillé* and he was asinine enough to make a declaration of love to her. As a woman of the world, and of her century, Mme Dupin subjected Rousseau to a period of cold-ness, gave him some good advice and invited him to act as tem-porary tutor to her son, Dupin de Chenonceaux. Her stepson, Dupin de Francueil, became a close friend of Rousseau through their joint love of music and interest in chemistry. Rousseau moved from his wretched hotel to the Jeu de Paume in the rue Verdelet, which ran into the rue Plâtrière, where the Dupin house was. Then he caught inflammation of the lungs, and during his convalescence started to write a ballet entitled *Les Muses galantes,* which was subsequently successfully performed. On 26 June 1743, he was invited to become secretary to the French Ambassador in Venice, Comte Pierre-François de Montaigu, and accepted.

Through Lyons and down the Rhône, with a quick visit to Mme de Warens at Chambéry, Rousseau reached Marseilles and embarked for Genoa, where he was kept in quarantine for twelve days. On 4 September he arrived in Venice. He lived at the embassy, Palazzo Toma Quirini, on the Fondamenta delle Peni-tente, by the Canareggio. From the start, things went badly be-tween the Ambassador and his secretary, who was peeved to be told

Madame Dupin, the Parisian hostess who invited Rousseau to be tutor to her son and employed him as her secretary. Her husband was a grandson of the Maréchal de Saxe and she was the grandmother of Aurore Dupin, Baronne Dudevant, better known as George Sand

Rousseau as secretary to the Comte de Montaigu, Ambassador of France in Venice, in 1743. His appointment was a disaster and ended with an open breach between them

that he was secretary to the Ambassador, not to the embassy. None the less, it was Rousseau who wrote the dispatches to the King of France or to the secretaries of state, and notes to the Senate of the Most Serene Republic of Venice.

Rousseau's time was not exclusively occupied with secretarial work. In Casanova's own home-town, it was inevitable that Rousseau should taste its great speciality, the courtesans. With La Padoana there was a scene which showed again the passive part that Rousseau played in amorous matters. After drinking her sorbets and hearing her sing, he put a ducat on the table and prepared to leave, but she refused to accept it unless she earned it.

Venice, entrance to the Canareggio, the canal on the banks of which stood the French Embassy in the Palazzo Toma Quirini, Fondamenta delle Penitente. Rousseau lived in the Embassy

He could not understand afterwards why he had not become infected. The second occasion was even more significant. The image that he had conjured up for himself of the passionate pleasure that Zulietta would afford him was not realized. On entering her room, and seeing her in *vestito di confidenza,* it was either the thought that she really belonged to another man, or the discovery that one of her breasts had no nipple, that resulted in his collapse into floods of tears. The whore added to his discomfiture by saying, 'Johnny, leave women and study mathematics.'

The breach with the Ambassador became open when the latter told Rousseau that there would be no place at table for Rousseau when

Venice, a courtyard. The beauties and wonders of Venice were spoilt for Rousseau by the constant hostility between him and his master, the Ambassador, and his amorous adventures were an arrant failure

the Duke of Modena and his suite came to dinner. Rousseau remonstrated firmly, but without effect. In the event, the Duke of Modena did not come to dinner. Among Rousseau's other complaints, in addition to constant humiliation by his very rank-conscious but incompetent Ambassador, were the withdrawal of his personal gondola, and the irregular payment of his salary and expenses. After a furious scene on 6 August 1744, Rousseau left the embassy in disgrace and called on his friend the French Consul to tell him the whole story. The Consul kept him to dinner, which happened to be attended by all the French notabilities in Venice. The Ambassador had nobody at his table, and this made him so

26

angry that he sent a note to the Venetian Senate asking for Rousseau's arrest. That august body proceeded with sufficient dignity to do nothing until Rousseau had left Venice on 22 August. But none of all this storm was lost on Rousseau in forming his opinion of high French society and of the 'establishment'.

Rousseau returned from Venice by the Simplon pass, and on the way admired greatly the Borromean Islands which were to occupy his thoughts later. In Paris he stayed first at the Hôtel d'Orléans, rue du Chantre, near the Palais Royal; next with a Spanish friend in the rue Saint-Honoré; and finally in his old haunt, the Hôtel Saint-Quentin. His attempts to recover the money which he claimed was owed to him by the Ambassador in Venice were rebuffed on the grounds that he was not a French subject and therefore had no redress. He even wrote to the Minister for Foreign Affairs, begging for 'justice', in vain, of course, but in his letter there appeared for the first time a theme that was to obsess him for the rest of his life. He wanted justification not only for himself and his self-esteem, but also in order that the 'public' should not despise him, victim of injustice. Meanwhile, he finished his ballet, *Les Muses galantes,* which was performed in September 1745 at the house of the controller of ceremonies and theatrical performances, at Passy. This was some consolation.

For the celebrations of the wedding of the Dauphin, Voltaire and Rameau had been commissioned to write and compose a comedy

Venice, the Grand Canal. One of the many grievances of Rousseau with the Ambassador was that the latter had deprived him of the use of a personal gondola which he had previously enjoyed

The *bal masque* held at Versailles for the marriage of the Dauphin. The ballet for these celebrations had been written by Voltaire and set to music by Jean-Philippe Rameau, as *La Princesse de Navarre*, in three acts. Voltaire shortened the script to one act and Rousseau was commissioned to shorten the music, but was neither thanked nor paid for his work

ballet, *La Princesse de Navarre,* which they did, in three acts. The Duc de Richelieu wanted these to be reduced to one act, and Voltaire quickly rewrote the script as *Les Fêtes de Ramire.* But the music also had to be made to conform, and Richelieu commissioned Rousseau to do this. The piece was performed at Versailles on 22 December 1745. Although he had done the ungrateful work of seamster, Rousseau was not even mentioned in the programme and received no payment. He made himself ill with chagrin.

The Hôtel Saint-Quentin had engaged a washerwoman, Thérèse Levasseur, from Orléans. She also waited at table and was mocked by the guests for her country manners. This was enough to put Rousseau on her side. Thirteen years younger than he, she became his mistress and he promised that he would never abandon her nor ever marry her. He kept the first promise but not the second. She was illiterate and for a man who thought that he had reached the level of embassy secretary, it showed that his aims in society were beginning to change. She had five children by him, each taken by the midwife to the foundling hospital. In a letter written in cipher to Mme de Francueil, he justified his behaviour on a number of grounds. First, he was incurably ill from retention of urine, owing to urethral constriction and loss of tone in the bladder-muscles, and he feared that he would not live long. He had no fortune or stable profession that would enable him to bring up his children, or to bequeath anything to them. If the Levasseur family brought them up they would become 'little monsters'. Finally, in the foundling hospital, not being pampered, they would fare better; and this was the way that Plato's *Republic* recommended children should be brought up, by the state. In December 1747, Rousseau and Thérèse set up house at the Hôtel du Saint-Esprit, rue Plâtrière.

It was not unusual in Paris for illegitimate children to be abandoned by their parents. Mme du Tencin had a son who was exposed at the door of the church of Saint Jean-le-Rond; he was given this name and later added d'Alembert. Rousseau and d'Alembert met in 1746, at the time when d'Alembert and Diderot were starting to organize the production of the *Encyclopédie, dictionnaire raisonné des sciences, des arts et des métiers*. This was a task for which they were well qualified, d'Alembert being a great mathematician and physicist and Diderot a fountain of ideas on biology. It had originally been intended that the *Encyclopédie* should be a translation of Ephraim Chambers's *Cyclopaedia*, published in London in 1728; but so much progress had been made in science and technology since that date that they decided to start again, from scratch.

Privilege to publish the *Encyclopédie* was given on 21 January 1746 and the first volume was published in 1751. Rousseau was invited to contribute the articles on Music and on Political

(*Left*) The Hôtel du Saint-Esprit, in the rue Plâtrière (now rue Jean-Jacques Rousseau) where Rousseau and Thérèse set up house

(*Right*) Sisters of St Vincent de Paul caring for foundlings in the Paris Foundling Hospital, to which Rousseau's children were taken

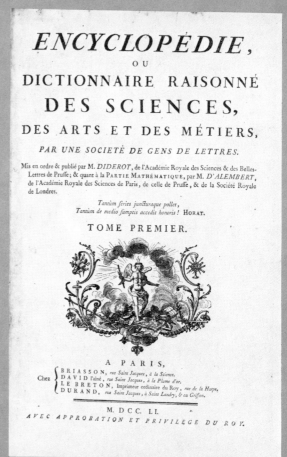

Frontispiece and title-page of the first volume of the *Encyclopédie* published in 1751, edited by Diderot. This dictionary of science and technology encountered increasing opposition because of its 'materialism', and its publication was for some time suspended

Economy. The *Encyclopédie* soon began to encounter opposition because of its tendency 'to support materialism, destroy religion, and encourage independence', as the French Attorney-General complained. D'Alembert thought it wiser to withdraw into the background and the work was carried through entirely by Diderot who, with his collaborators, formed a group who became known as the *philosophes*.

Denis Diderot, son of a cutler of Langres, was one of the most penetrating thinkers and writers of the century. His central belief was in the pre-eminence of nature. He did not accept that there was a God in nature, but held that the universe was a field in which little bits of matter pushed one another about. This faith in naturalism led him to reject Christian morality, because it opposed natural pleasures arising from natural functions. He therefore rejected the so-called virtues such as chastity, modesty and sobriety, which refer only to the individual. The real virtue, according to him, was charity, applied to all humanity, to the benefit of which science and technology must be devoted.

In June 1749, Diderot published an essay, *Lettre sur les aveugles,* based on the life of the Cambridge professor of mathematics Nicholas Saunderson, who became totally blind when one year old. Diderot developed the theme that arguments in favour of the existence of God, drawn from the marvels of nature, do not mean much to a blind man. 'If you want me to believe in God you must make me touch him.' This was a direct attack on the supposedly inexhaustible compassion of the Almighty, and an argument for materialism, quite sufficient for Diderot to be thrown into the dungeon of the Château de Vincennes on 24 July 1749, without trial. Rousseau was so upset at this treatment of his friend that, with a mixture of obsequiousness and effrontery, soon to become usual with him, he wrote to Mme de Pompadour to ask that Diderot be freed, or that he, Rousseau, be imprisoned with him.

(*Above*) Denis Diderot, editor and chief author of the *Encyclopédie*. His *Lettre sur les aveugles* was considered to be so blasphemous that he was thrown into the dungeon of the Château de Vincennes on 24 July 1749

(*Left*) The donjon of the Château de Vincennes near Paris, a fourteenth-century fortress, where Diderot was imprisoned. On his way to visit Diderot in prison Rousseau had his 'revelation' that progress in arts and sciences was disastrous for mankind

A month later, the conditions of Diderot's detention were relaxed and in October Rousseau went to visit him, still in prison. On the walk from Paris to Vincennes, he read a newspaper and saw an announcement that the Academy of Dijon offered a prize for the best essay on whether the re-establishment of arts and sciences had contributed to the improvement of morals. In proposing a competition on such a subject in the middle of the century of Enlightenment, the academicians of Dijon could hardly have guessed that they were starting something that has not stopped even now. To Rousseau the question was a revelation; in a flash he saw that the answer to it solved all his problems. It revealed himself to himself and let him taste the sweetness of the revenge that he would take over the injustices he had suffered. He would answer the question with an unqualified NO.

It was progress in the arts and sciences which had produced the artificial and vicious world in which society heaped riches, privileges and honours on those who possessed property and inflicted every kind of hardship and misery on those who had none. Furthermore, while the rich prided themselves on their manners, vanities and degraded habits, they were riddled with vice. 'Our souls have been corrupted to the extent that the arts and sciences have progressed towards perfection.' Whence can these abuses have come, except from the fatal inequality which man introduced, with consequent debasement of virtue? War on inequality was to become Rousseau's key-thought.

In his *Discours sur les sciences et les arts*, the invention of printing came in for special condemnation. By its means the dangerous dreams of Thomas Hobbes, who did not believe in the primitive virtue of man, will be preserved to all posterity. Omar had ordered the burning of the library of Alexandria. If Gregory the Great had been in the place of Omar, and the Gospels in that of the Koran, would the result have been different? Rulers should be as keen to forbid printing in their kingdoms as they had been to introduce it.

The most blessed times that mankind experienced were when cities, arts, sciences and technology did not exist, before they had brought luxury, laxity of morals and slavery into society, punishments self-inflicted by man's conceited efforts to get out of the happy state of ignorance in which eternal wisdom had placed him in nature. A man who thinks is a depraved animal. Astronomy was born of superstition; eloquence of ambition, lies, hatred and flattery; geometry of avarice; physics of vain curiosity. All these sciences stem from human vanity; arts and sciences are a product of our vices. Of what use could the arts be if there were no luxury on which to feed; or history without tyrants, wars and conspiracies?

Rousseau's paradox was awarded the prize and published. The examiners can hardly have come to their decision on the merits of

(*Left*) An example of the injustices of society against which Rousseau campaigned: a lady of high aristocracy soliciting a judge

(*Below*) A state of nature was Rousseau's ideal, when cities, luxury, arts and sciences did not exist. This painting by William Hodges in New Zealand in 1777 would have delighted Rousseau's heart

the thesis, and must have been impressed by the beauty of its prose style, the originality of its ideas and perhaps its scandal-value. The result was, however, that from the day of its publication, Rousseau leapt into fame. In spite of his later denials, this was exactly what his vanity hungered for. But there was another effect, even more serious, which was to last until the end of his life; the man had become the prisoner of the author, and had to keep up the paradox until the day of his death. In this first *Discours* it was no mean feat to write a book to prove that literature is nothing but harmful vanity. The same basic contradiction will be found in all Rousseau's later works, on the theatre, marital relations, education and political institutions.

In January 1750, Rousseau and Thérèse moved to the Hôtel du Languedoc, rue de Grenelle-Saint-Honoré. He was in a fair way to making a successful career for himself, with a wide circle of cultured and influential friends. He lived on three levels. With the Dupins, from whom he was earning a good salary as secretary and cashier, he enjoyed the luxury of their house in Paris and the beautiful Château de Chenonceaux on the Loire. Every week he took his midday meal with Diderot and Condillac at the Panier Fleuri in the Palais Royal, discussing philosophy. In the evenings he had supper in the somewhat squalid lodgings of the Levasseur family, at the end of the rue Saint-Jacques. But he felt that this could not go on and that as a man who had publicly pilloried the vicious rich

Specimen of music copied by Rousseau. After he had resigned from his employment with Madame Dupin, Rousseau earned his living by copying music for which he was paid ten *sous* a page

34

and society as a whole, he must practise what he preached. He therefore resigned from his salaried appointments to the Dupins; it was the first time that he had given notice; till then it had always been given to him. To earn his bread he returned to an expedient that had once saved him in Lyons: he copied music at ten *sous* a page. There was still demand for work of this kind, for the different parts of orchestras and for the voices of choirs.

This was only the first stage of his 'reform'. He had become a *citoyen* but was still on good terms with his rich friends. Meanwhile he returned to his beloved music and composed an opera, *Le Devin du village* (The Village Soothsayer), which was performed on 18 October 1752 at Fontainebleau, before Louis XV and the court. He was to have an audience of the King on the following day, and perhaps to have a royal pension allotted to him, but he left Fontainebleau before the audience was to be held. His urinary trouble made him increasingly shy of attending any grand function from which he could not retire at quick need.

Le Devin du village had considerable success when performed in Paris and the Théâtre Français put on his *Narcisse, ou l'amant de lui-même*, the text of which had been touched up for him by the poet

(*Left*) Title-page of Rousseau's operetta *Le Devin du village*, published in 1753. It was performed at Fontainebleau before Louis XV and the Court on 18 October 1752

(*Right*) Engraving from *Le Devin du village* showing two of the characters, Colette and the soothsayer

Illustration from Rousseau's opera *Narcisse, ou l'amant de lui-même*, published in 1753. He had first written it some fifteen years before, and the text was touched up for him by the poet Marivaux. Rousseau gave it a new preface in which he renewed his onslaught against arts and sciences, including literature, music and drama. As he himself contributed to each of these forms of art, he defended himself by saying that while he might be behaving badly in doing so, arts and sciences were nevertheless nefarious

Marivaux. In 1753 Rousseau printed it, with a new preface in which he took up again his onslaught against arts and sciences, and against those who accused him of inconsistency in preaching their devastating effects while practising them in literature, music and drama. His defence was a masterpiece of dialectical casuistry. If the sentiments of men were to be deduced from their actions, there could be no Christians on earth. Intention was what counted, not action. Armed with this wonderful passport, Rousseau claimed that while he might be behaving badly in writing books and plays, this did not mean that his principle of condemning books and plays was wrong. This sophistry was on a par with his reversal of the normal practice of judging a man's character by his works; on the contrary, said Rousseau, his works were to be judged by his character which was, of course, 'good'. With these internal contradictions and inconsistencies justified, he was cheating against himself, and was to continue doing so more and more.

Less successful was another excursion into music when Rousseau published *Lettre sur la musique française*, in 1753. It was the old story of his preference for melody over harmony, and therefore for Italian rather than French music. Indeed, in his *Lettre*, the latter with its complicated harmony is maligned. 'French song is nothing but a continuous bark.' This outburst did him no good. On the one hand, the question was asked, what right has this Swiss to speak of French music as 'our music'; on the other, the orchestra of the Paris Opéra hanged him in effigy and he was refused the entry to it that he had enjoyed.

DISCOURS

*SUR L'ORIGINE ET LES FONDEMENS
DE L'INEGALITÉ PARMI LES HOMMES.*

Par JEAN JAQUES ROUSSEAU

CITOYEN DE GENÈVE.

Non in depravatis, fed in his quæ bene fecundum
naturam fe habent, confiderandum eft quid fit na-
turale. ARISTOT. Politic. L. 2.

A AMSTERDAM,

Chez MARC MICHEL REY.

M D C C L V.

Title-page to Rousseau's *Essay on the Origin and Foundation of Inequality between Men,* published in 1755. This was Rousseau's entry for a prize competition offered by the Academy of Dijon in 1753, in which he was able to extend and expand the views advanced by him in his entry for a prize competition offered by the same Academy in 1749, when he contended that progress in arts and sciences had been disastrous for mankind. The views expressed in these two *Discours* held him in their grip for the rest of his life

In the same year, 1753, the Academy of Dijon announced another prize competition, for an essay on the subject of the origin of inequality among men, and whether it was sanctioned by natural law. This gave Rousseau an unexpected opportunity to extend the thesis he had put forward in his first *Discours* and to expand his condemnation of the vice and wickedness of society. This deserves detailed consideration, for it coloured everything that he afterwards wrote, always with himself as term of reference. It is easiest to describe the *Discours sur l'origine de l'inégalité parmi les hommes* by quoting half a dozen of the propositions he laid down, and seeing what they are worth.

LES ILLUSTRES FRANÇAIS.

Allegorical portrait of Georges Louis Leclerc, Comte de Buffon, author of the *Histoire naturelle*, a landmark in biology and also in literature for which Buffon became a member of the Académie Française. In this work Buffon described apes as living in bands, but Rousseau failed to notice the significance of this fact for the origin of the social state

The start was unpromising, for Rousseau prefaced his work with the words, 'Let us begin by discarding all the facts, because they do not bear on the question.' Admittedly, few facts were established at that time about the conditions under which primitive man lived, but there were some, which Rousseau brushed aside and for which he substituted products of his own imagination. These, applied to primitive man, led him to assert that 'In this primitive state, without houses, huts, or property of any kind, each individual finding a lodging haphazard, often only for a single night, males and females met and mated by accident, in accordance with luck, occasion, and desire.'

Rousseau's condemnation of society obliged him to believe that man was originally non-social. It is curious that he paid no attention to Buffon's description of apes as going about in bands of several individuals living together, which should have suggested to him that man's ancestors were already social animals before they ever became men at all.

Rousseau's absurd and monstrous assertion that a woman, when pregnant by a man, had no more reason to need his company after

38

childbirth than before she chanced to meet him, had already been exposed as untrue by John Locke. In the latter's *Treatises of Government* published in 1690, he showed that the association between a man and a woman was not solely for the purpose of procreation, but must last at least as long as necessary for the weaning and teaching of the newborn until it was capable of meeting its own needs. Rousseau knew of Locke's work and rejected it by the worst form of circular argument, saying, 'Although it may be advantageous to the human species that the union between a man and a woman be permanent, it does not follow that this was established by nature; otherwise it would be necessary to say that nature has also instituted civilized society, arts, trade and everything held to be useful to men.' In other words, Locke's sound biology must be wrong because Rousseau's views on society must be right.

'Men, by common consent, are by nature as equal to one another as are animals of the same species.' This assertion is disproved by genetics and by ethology, which has shown that populations of higher animals have instinctive hierarchies, or 'pecking orders', allowing them different priorities as regards occupation of territory, securing mates and obtaining food. There is every reason to suppose that primitive man was similar to these animals.

'I shall ask what solid evidence there is that in countries where the art of medicine is least practised, the expectation of life is shorter than in countries where it is most assiduously pursued . . . . With so few sources of ills, man in a state of nature needs no remedies and fewer doctors.' It is perhaps unfair to quote back at Rousseau the statistics drawn up by the United Nations: in 1962 the expectation of life for male births in Great Britain was 68 years, 45 in India and 30 in Guinea. But it is fair to object that malaria, trypanosomiasis, bilharziasis and many other diseases, as well as famine, have been checked by progress in medicine, dietetics, agriculture and fisheries, none of which Rousseau's savages would have had. Nor is he on any firmer ground in claiming absence of disease in animals and primitive man. Fossils give plenty of evidence of monstrosities, arthritis, osteitis, dental caries, etc.

'Commiseration will be all the stronger from the fact that the animal spectator identifies himself more intimately with the suffering animal . . . . It is therefore certain that pity is a natural sentiment.' The poet William Cowper had three hares and noticed that, when one of them was ill, the other two went for it and increased its sufferings. Darwin reported the same in cattle of the Chillingham herd, and any careful observer of mammals and birds in nature can see it happening. Evidence from the earliest stages of human evolution is no different. The skull of the Palaeolithic Man of Monte Circeo shows that he was killed and beheaded, and his brain-case broken open, doubtless to extract the brain and eat it. The same is found in Peking Man, in Neanderthal Man from Krapina, Ehringsdorf, Ngandang and Steinheim, and the Bronze Age Man of Wansleben. The Man of Tolund was strangled. It is possible that some of these cases of violence were based on religious rituals or human sacrifice, like that seen in the rock-drawings in the cave at Addaura near Palermo, but they provide a complete refutation of Rousseau's assertion of the natural sentiment of pity.

'The first who enclosed a piece of ground and said "this is mine", and found others simple enough to believe him, was the true founder of civilized society.' Here, Rousseau was on his target, but he was utterly ignorant of who that first malefactor was, to claim ownership of territory. This instinct is natural in animals, and particularly well developed in birds and mammals, where mated couples need territory extensive enough to provide food for their young, and advertise their ownership by song (in birds), and by deposits of excrement and urine on its boundary (in mammals).

The imaginative fancies on which Rousseau based his system that man is naturally 'good' but became vitiated by civilized society, are all wrong in fact. Nobody can construct a conjectural history of primitive man without knowledge of biology, anthropology and sociology; and Rousseau was ignorant of them all. His second *Discours* also reveals his faulty methodology. Given, as he was, to making arbitrary assertions, he would have been horrified if the great Bossuet's words had been quoted against him: 'The greatest error of the mind is to believe things because one wants them to be so, and not because one has seen them to be so' (*Traité de la connaissance de Dieu et de soi-même*, 1, 16). Nor would Rousseau have relished Oliver Cromwell's reply to the Scottish Commissioners: 'I beseech you in the bowels of Christ to consider it possible that ye may be mistaken.' Rousseau was absolutely convinced that what he said, thought, asserted, claimed or preached, was right.

Like many other men, Rousseau became intoxicated by his own propaganda. This explains his certitude of correctness. Having to his own satisfaction shown that, before civilization ruined him, man was virtuous and free, he claimed this virtue for himself because he had cleansed himself from the vices of society by his 'reform', and thereby regained natural 'goodness'. His great complaint was that he was not allowed 'natural freedom'. This moral absolution that he gave himself went a long way.

Among the countless comments that Rousseau's second *Discours* invites, there is one of great importance. As he said himself, he discarded facts and replaced them by what he thought were arguments, but which were only figments of his imagination. There can seldom have been a man with more powers of imagination than he. Ever since his adolescence, as he admitted, he practised masturbation, and the imaginary partners of his daydreams gave him more satisfaction than real female flesh and blood, because the former excelled in all the virtues and qualities that he wanted a woman to have. But while his imagination worked overtime to provide him with pleasures that he could rarely get from his senses, or from recollections of his friends, and of places where he had been happy, his imagination, in a constant state of effervescence, also worked in the opposite direction. With increasing scope as he grew older, it conjured up fears and phobias of illnesses, or of enemies conspiring against him to deprive him of his freedom and rights or, worst of all, to produce fictitious and malevolent deformations of his works and thoughts, and to pass them off as his own, in order to discredit him in the eyes of posterity.

In 1754, Rousseau felt that his 'reform' required that he identify himself again with his birthplace, in its simplicity and virtue. He decided to dedicate his second *Discours* to the Republic of Geneva, and had it printed. (It did not, incidentally, win the Dijon prize.) He must shake off the Roman Catholicism that he had superficially adopted. He and Thérèse set off and on the way they paid a visit to Mme de Warens at Chambéry. She was in a poor way and declining. Her efforts to establish a soap factory had failed, as had her iron- and coal-mines. In after years, Rousseau did not forgive himself for abandoning Mme de Warens at that time, when she was in such great want and distress.

In Geneva, Rousseau was catechized by the pastors, whom he satisfied but not without some difficulty and some condescension on their part, because of Thérèse. She could show no marriage lines and she slept in his bedroom. The difficulty was avoided on the plea that her presence was continuously necessary to nurse his incurable illness of retention of urine. On 1 August 1754, he was readmitted to the Calvinist Church and by the same token recovered his rights as citizen of Geneva.

In September, with some friends, he and Thérèse made a tour by boat of the Lake of Geneva: Coudrée, Meillerie, Vevey, Lausanne, Morges and Nyon were the stopping-places before returning to Geneva. In 1816, Shelley and Byron were to make a similar tour as a pilgrimage to places hallowed by Rousseau. In spite of all his professed preference for the country over towns, Rousseau was really a townsman, and this tour enabled him to collect 'material', particularly of the eastern end of the lake, Meillerie, Clarens and the shore of the Pays de Vaud.

Rousseau's pilgrimage to Geneva was more significant than a simple act of patriotism and filial piety; it throws light on some basic features of his life and work. For a hundred and fifty years, his ancestors in Geneva had lived in an atmosphere of Calvinist religion and republican democracy, completely sheltered from the blossoming of French literary genius in the seventeenth century,

View on the Lake of Geneva, in which can be seen the ideals which Rousseau extolled: nature unspoilt, pastoral scenes, peasants, cottages; no cities, factories or luxury; an antithesis which Rousseau was to develop in his books *La nouvelle Héloïse* and *Émile*. Rousseau made a tour of the lake in 1754 refreshing his memory of scenes of his youth

with its Corneille, Molière and Racine. The Age of Enlightenment in the eighteenth century was the product of the work of these predecessors, but French high society took advantage of it to revel in irreligion and immorality. There was little music in Geneva, although many members of Rousseau's family had a liking for it. It could almost have been predicted how the lower middle-class republican from Geneva would react when he plunged into the literary and musical brilliance of life in Paris, in the absolute monarchy of France. What could not have been predicted was the genius which this French environment would evoke in Rousseau.

In the following year, 1755, Voltaire established himself at Geneva, in a fine house that he called Les Délices. It was also the year when Rousseau's second *Discours* was published, and he sent a copy to Voltaire, who replied, on 30 August 1755, 'Sir, I have received your new book, written against the human race, and I thank you.... Never was so much intelligence used to make us stupid. While reading it, one longs to go on all fours.' Rousseau returned a soft answer, but the seeds of enmity had been sown between the two men. The fact that Voltaire had settled in Geneva, which Rousseau was always to regard as his city, was a hard blow to him and decided him not to return there. Relations between the two men became even more strained after the Lisbon earthquake in 1755, about which Voltaire wrote a poem, rejecting the optimistic

(*Left*) Voltaire. The artist, Théodore Gardelle, was hanged in front of the door of his lodgings in London for raping his landlady's daughter

(*Right*) 'The kicks', illustration from Voltaire's *Candide*, written after the Lisbon earthquake of 1755 to ridicule the view that 'everything is for the best'

principle that everything is for the best in the best of all worlds possible and urging the recognition of the existence of evil. Rousseau replied with a *Lettre sur la providence*, dated 18 August 1756, protesting politely against Voltaire's rejection of the goodness of providence and the implication that God had placed Man on earth only to suffer. Voltaire's indirect reply was his masterpiece, *Candide*.

In 1756, Dr Théodore Tronchin, the celebrated physician, offered Rousseau the post of honorary librarian in the city of Geneva. Rousseau refused it and, instead, carried out the second stage of his 'reform'. He had to some extent still been running with the hares and hunting with the hounds. Now that he was clear what his position, his abilities and his aims were, it was time for him to show his distaste for cities and assert his independence by retiring into the country. He had been introduced some years previously to Mme d'Épinay by her lover, Dupin de Francueil, his own friend. The wife of a *fermier-général* and very rich, she owned a château near the forest of Montmorency and also a house close by, called l'Hermitage, which she furnished and offered to Rousseau. Boorishly he replied to Mme d'Épinay that she was mistaken if she thought that she could turn a friend into a flunkey; he was not for sale and insisted on maintaining his complete independence. Eventually, however, he accepted on condition that no gratitude was involved on his part. He had decided that friendship was incompatible with gratitude

43

Madame d'Épinay, Rousseau's benefactress and subsequent enemy

L'Hermitage at Montmorency, the house which Mme d'Épinay lent to Rousseau and where he began to write his most important books

and that, as friendship was the more important, he must never owe anything to anybody. This meant that his ingratitude was part of a doctrine, more and more rigidly enforced as people showed him kindnesses during the rest of his life. This is the explanation of much of his later behaviour. He craved sympathy and affection, but with the same breath he rejected both. In the present case, Mme d'Épinay laughed and called him 'My Bear' – she might have added, 'with a sore head'. On 9 April 1756, her coach fetched Rousseau, Thérèse and her mother, Mme Levasseur, and they settled in at l'Hermitage.

In his beautiful country retreat, from which he could wander to his heart's content in the forest of Montmorency, Rousseau entered his most productive period and started writing his most important books. Walking in the forest, he spent his time in daydreams, creating out of his imagination the characters who were to figure in his novel, *Julie, ou la nouvelle Héloïse*. They were Julie d'Étanges and her cousin Claire d'Orbe, possessed of every quality of charm and virtue. During a long absence of Julie's father, Baron d'Étanges, her mother invites into the house a young man of modest origins, Saint-Preux, who acts as tutor to Julie. He gives her lessons, but he also seduces her, as Abélard seduced Héloïse, whence the full title of Rousseau's book. When Baron d'Étanges returns, he approves of the progress that Julie has made with her studies, but will not hear of being indebted to a plebeian tutor. Saint-Preux, for his part, refuses to accept any salary, which would make him a servant.

Hopelessly in love, Saint-Preux and Julie exchange interminable letters, wallowing in sentimentality and emotion. An unlikely

Englishman appears, Lord Edward Bomston, who also falls in love with Julie. He and Saint-Preux prepare to fight a duel, but milord, who is drunk, sprains his ankle, and the fight is postponed. When Lord Edward learns of Julie's love for Saint-Preux, he goes to Baron d'Étanges and pleads for Julie's hand, not for himself, but for Saint-Preux. The baron has other ideas. Inordinately rank-conscious, he will not hear of his daughter marrying a common man, but insists on her betrothal to his friend M. de Wolmar, a Hungarian nobleman who once saved his life. Julie is not complaisant, her father boxes her ears, she falls and hurts herself on a table and, by good fortune, has a miscarriage.

Julie then bows to her father's wishes and marries M. de Wolmar, without any love for him. Meanwhile, Saint-Preux who has gone to England with Lord Edward, sails round the world with Admiral Anson. Wolmar's tender kindness conquers Julie's love so that when Saint-Preux returns, some years later, he finds a blissfully happy married couple, with two children, living in a hamlet, Clarens, by the Lake of Geneva. Wolmar knows all about the past, but invites Saint-Preux to come and live with them. He comes and is captivated by the simplicity and devoted love of the couple. Julie wants him to act as tutor to her children and hopes that he will marry her cousin Claire d'Orbe. Saint-Preux exclaims, 'Julie, there are eternal impressions which time and care do not efface. The wound heals, but the scar remains.' One of Julie's children falls into the lake and Julie plunges into the water to save it, but catches pleurisy from which she dies: the supreme sacrifice of maternal love.

(*Left*) Rousseau's *La nouvelle Héloïse* had so great a success that illustrated editions of the novel were published. This, 'The first kiss of love', shows the tutor Saint-Preux with his beloved Julie d'Étanges and her cousin Claire d'Orbe

(*Right*) 'Maternal love': Julie, now Mme de Wolmar, plunges into the lake to save her child, but as a result of this action she catches pleurisy and dies

(*Right*) The forest of Montmorency, where Rousseau roamed while thinking out and writing *La nouvelle Héloïse*, showing the chestnut tree in the foreground popularly associated with Rousseau

(*Below*) 'The monuments to old loves': Saint-Preux shows Julie de Wolmar the marks of their former visit to Meillerie, opposite Clarens

(*Above*) The Borromean Islands on Lake Maggiore, where for a time Rousseau thought of setting the scene of *La nouvelle Héloïse*

(*Right*) Robinson Crusoe saving his goods out of the wreck of the ship. Defoe's work was one of Rousseau's favourite books because of his longing for the seclusion of an isolated island

Clarens on the Lake of Geneva, where Rousseau set the scene for *La nouvelle Héloïse*. On the hill is Le Châtelard, original seat of Mme de Warens's family, which was the reason why Rousseau placed his novel there

The aim of the book was to show that the majesty of virtue and married bliss could prevail over the immorality and promiscuity which was prevalent in Paris, where every lady of quality had a lover and every gentleman a mistress. With the deliberate intention of denigrating society and city life, the action takes place as far from a big city as possible; not even in France, but in a small village in Switzerland, where the inhabitants have been least contaminated by arts and sciences. The setting of the scene was the result of some hesitation on Rousseau's part, because of his liking for islands, refuges of isolation and solitude. *Robinson Crusoe* was one of his favourite books, and on his voyage, Saint-Preux is made to sail between the isolated islands of Juan Fernandez and Tinian. On his return from Venice, Rousseau saw the Borromean Islands and, as he required a lake for the end of his novel, he thought for a time of placing it there, on Lago Maggiore. He decided in favour of Clarens and the Lake of Geneva because it was the original home of Mme de Warens.

Mme d'Épinay had introduced Rousseau to her sister-in-law, the Comtesse d'Houdetot, who had a house near by. She had a lover, the Marquis de Saint-Lambert who, with her husband, went away to the war in Germany. When Mme d'Houdetot called on Rousseau wearing riding-breeches and carrying a riding-crop, he fell head over heels in love with her and saw her with the eyes of Saint-Preux seeing Julie. The letters from Saint-Preux to Julie were really those from Rousseau to his perfect dream-woman; those from Julie to Saint-Preux were the letters that Rousseau imagined his dream-woman would write to him: no real woman ever had. While writing his book, he was in a heaven no less real to him for

*Comment peux-tu te resoudre à détruire ainsi ton propre ouvrage?
Comment oses-tu rendre indigne de ton estime celui qui fut
honoré de tes bontés? Ah Sophie! je t'en conjure, ne te fais point
rougir de l'ami que tu as recherché. C'est pour ta propre gloire
que je te demande compte de moi. Ne suis-je pas ton bien? N'en
as-tu pas pris possession? Tu ne peux plus t'en dédire, et puisque
je t'appartiens malgré moi-même et malgré toi, laisse-moi du
moins mériter de t'appartenir. Rappelle-toi ces tems de félicité
qui pour mon tourment ne sortiront jamais de ma mémoire.
Cette flamme vivifiante dont je reçus une seconde vie plus
précieuse que la première, rendoit à mon ame ainsi qu'à mes
sens toute la vigueur de la jeunesse: l'ardeur de mes sentimens
m'élevoit jusqu'à toi: combien de fois ton coeur plein d'un autre
amour fut-il ému des transports du mien? Combien de fois
m'as-tu dit dans le bosquet de la cascade: vous êtes l'amant le
plus tendre dont ...*

Draft of a letter from Rousseau to Madame d'Houdetot. Written in the intimacy of the second person singular, its contents make it easy to see why the Comtesse burnt Rousseau's letters to her when her husband (and her lover, Saint-Lambert) returned from the war in Germany

being a product of his imagination. But now, with Mme d'Houdetot, he lived his own novel, just staying within the bounds of propriety. But Mme d'Houdetot's husband and lover returned from the war; she hastily burnt Rousseau's letters to her, and asked Rousseau to return hers to him. As she was a countess and he only lower middle class, their affection was bound to founder on the rock of social status and make Rousseau feel still more humiliated.

Rousseau's withdrawal from Paris and his *philosophe* friends there caused a rift that was soon to become an open feud. Diderot, d'Alembert and Melchior Grimm, the influential editor of *La correspondance littéraire*, who had become a close friend of Rousseau, all considered that he had deserted the cause of progress. In Diderot's *Le fils naturel*, one passage said, 'The good man lives in society; it is only the wicked man who lives alone.' Rousseau took this as aimed on purpose at him.

Further trouble arose in connection with Mme d'Épinay, who was now Grimm's mistress. She had been advised to consult Dr Tronchin in Geneva, and Diderot considered that it was Rousseau's duty to escort her. He refused, partly invoking his illness. This led to acrimonious correspondence and ended in complete rupture. On 10 December 1757, Rousseau received from Mme d'Épinay a letter which he interpreted as a notice to quit and five days later he moved out. He was lucky enough to find another house, Mont-Louis, vacant close by.

In 1757 appeared the volume of the *Encyclopédie* which contained d'Alembert's article on Geneva, in which he drew attention

Mont-Louis, the house at Montmorency into which Rousseau moved after he had left L'Hermitage in December 1757. Mont-Louis belonged to M. Mathas, agent to the Prince de Condé

The summer-house in the garden at Mont-Louis, which Rousseau used as a writing-room for his *Contrat social* and his *Émile*. He called it his 'dungeon'

(*Above*) Jean-le-Rond d'Alembert, mathematician, physicist, and friend of Voltaire and Diderot

(*Right*) Title-page of Rousseau's *Lettre à M. D'Alembert* in which he fulminated against the proposal to open a theatre in Geneva. Rousseau took three weeks to write it in his 'dungeon' at Mont-Louis

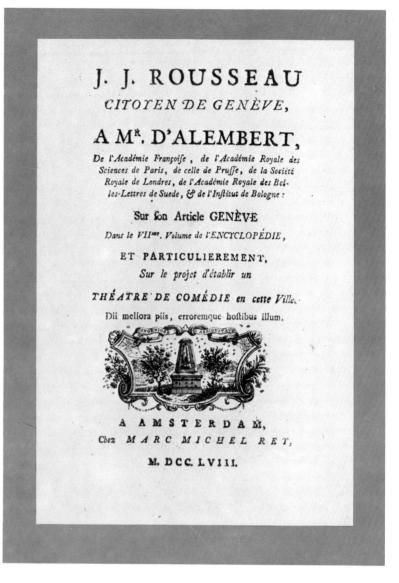

J. J. ROUSSEAU
CITOYEN DE GENÈVE,

A Mᴿ. D'ALEMBERT,

De l'Académie Françoise , de l'Académie Royale des Sciences de Paris, de celle de Prusse, de la Société Royale de Londres, de l'Académie Royale des Belles-Lettres de Suede, & de l'Institut de Bologne :

Sur son Article GENÈVE
Dans le VIIᵐᵉ. Volume de l'ENCYCLOPÉDIE,

ET PARTICULIEREMENT,
Sur le projet d'établir un

THÉATRE DE COMÉDIE *en cette Ville.*

Dii meliora piis, erroremque hostibus illum.

A AMSTERDAM,
Chez MARC MICHEL REY,

M. DCC. LVIII.

to the fact that the government of that city did not allow any theatres because of the supposedly built-in profligacy of actors and actresses. Voltaire was behind this; his actress friend, Adrienne Lecouvreur, had been refused Christian burial by the clergy of Paris, whereas Nan Oldfield had been buried in Westminster Abbey. If only Geneva would allow theatres, d'Alembert went on, with proper police safeguards against depravity, the taste of the citizens, their tact and delicate sentiments would be improved, foreigners would come on purpose to visit the city and trade would prosper.

This was more than Rousseau could bear. The theatre was one of the most pernicious products of society, its luxury and immorality, with which he was at war. He pitched headlong, burning with indignation, into his *Lettre à M. D'Alembert sur les spectacles*, which he finished in three weeks. The stage corrupts morals, he argued. What is the talent of an actor? The art of falsification and hypocrisy in assuming a character other than his own, and in saying things that he does not believe. What is the profession of an actor? A trade in which he exhibits himself for money. As for actresses, the finery of their apparel serves no purpose other than eroticism.

There follows a note on women which shows that Rousseau was riding a hobby-horse that had run away with him. 'In general, women like and appreciate no art and have no genius. They can succeed in small works that need only lightness of touch, thought and taste, and sometimes philosophy and reason.... Their writings are as cold and pretty as they are themselves, and contain as much wit as you like, but never a soul. They do not know how to describe or to feel the sentiment of love.'

Here, then, was a man who lived with a mistress and had had five illegitimate children, who had written a number of operas and plays, successfully performed, and who, in the name of morality, called down the wrath of heaven on the proposal that Geneva should have a theatre. Here, also, was a man who admitted to a passion for women, but maligned them wholesale, virtually denying that they had souls. All this was because of the principles that he had laid down in his two *Discours*, to which he must conform, and which were riding him to death. Lord Melbourne showed great insight when he said, 'Nobody ever did anything very foolish except from some strong principle.'

Rousseau's book earned him the undying hatred of Voltaire, who had set his heart on the establishment of a theatre in Geneva, where his own plays could be produced and he could act in them himself. In 1759, through a friend, he had offered Rousseau shelter in a house that he had bought, knowing perfectly well that Rousseau would refuse. But in the following year Rousseau learnt that his letter to Voltaire on providence had been published, and accused Voltaire of having done it. On 17 June 1760, Rousseau wrote Voltaire a letter which completed the rupture between the two men. Among other things, Rousseau said in his letter, 'I do not love you, Sir; you have hurt me where I am most sensitive, me, your disciple and enthusiastic supporter. You have ruined Geneva for the price of the shelter that you have there received. You have alienated my fellow citizens from me...you have made it impossible for me to live in my own city.... I hate you.' Voltaire did not reply, but wrote to a friend, 'I have received a long letter from Jean-Jacques Rousseau. He has gone quite mad. It is a pity.'

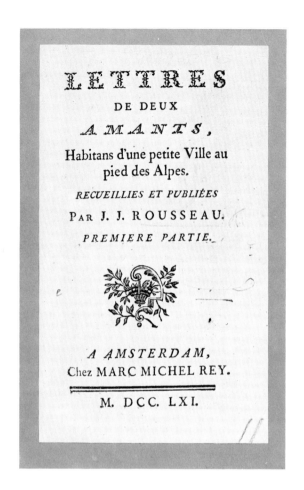

(*Above*) Title-page of an early edition of *La nouvelle Héloïse*, entitled 'Letters of two lovers, inhabitants of a small town at the foot of the Alps'

(*Right*) An illustration from Samuel Richardson's *Clarissa*. He had been the leading sentimental novelist, but on his death in July 1761 and the publication of *La nouvelle Héloïse* in that year, the title passed to Rousseau

After fulminating as he had against the moral corruption caused by drama and the stage, Rousseau felt obliged to say something to justify his publication of a novel, another medium for the under-mining of virtue. He did this in a second preface to *La nouvelle Héloïse*, in which he stressed that it was the virtue of country folk and not the apparatus of luxury that he was praising. His novel was therefore moral, and better than those of English writers, because these, like Samuel Richardson's *Clarissa*, preached to girls, whereas it was mothers who needed improvement.

La nouvelle Héloïse was published in 1761, and its immediate success was prodigious, helped by the death, in July of that year, of Samuel Richardson, whom Rousseau succeeded as the leading sentimental novelist. The descriptions of alpine pasturages (not of high mountains) in the Valais, excursions on the Lake of Geneva, the grape harvest at Clarens and the simplicity of the manners of the characters, were something new in a novel, as well as the fact that, for the first time, there was a book in which readers, particu-

An English artist's illustration for *La nouvelle Héloïse*, showing the vogue for Rousseau's novel in England

larly women, could identify themselves personally with the charac- ters. But it owed its phenomenal success chiefly to the eloquence and artistry of its prose, which has a musical quality not found in previous French books.

Rousseau's next book was *Du contrat social, ou principes du droit politique*, which was published in 1762. In it he was able to grind his axe further against society. As in his two *Discours*, he laid down his principles *a priori*. 'Man is born free, yet everywhere he is in chains. Why this change?' The making of political constitutions has been a problem ever since Plato. Political philosophy has varied in the extent to which the state claims power over its citizens and the citizens have freedom and rights of their own. Thomas Hobbes was less liberal to the citizen than John Locke in this respect, but Rousseau would have none of this restriction of individual liberty and rights. Unless a man has complete freedom, he is not a man. Rousseau gets round the problem ingeniously but disingenuously. In a perfect population there is a General Will, directed solely to

Rousseau with his *Contrat social*, apparently an English portrait

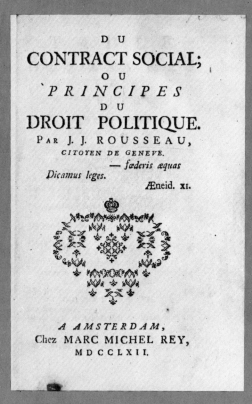

D U
CONTRACT SOCIAL;
O U
PRINCIPES
D U
DROIT POLITIQUE.
PAR J. J. ROUSSEAU,
CITOYEN DE GENEVE.
— *fœderis æquas*
Dicamus leges.
Æneid. XI.

A AMSTERDAM,
Chez MARC MICHEL REY,
MDCCLXII.

(*Right*) Title-page of Rousseau's *Contrat social*, his charter for social revolution

the common good. By associating himself with this General Will every man, although he loses his individual will, gains unlimited freedom and equal rights with everybody else.

Political parties are anathema because they represent Particular Wills, which can only hinder the General Will. Rousseau's non-party state is the caricature of a totalitarian one-party state. What happens if a man refuses to agree with the General Will? Here Rousseau remembers his Calvinist upbringing and the passage in the Old Testament, Numbers xv: 35, where Moses asks Jehovah what is to be done with a man found gathering sticks on the sabbath, and Jehovah himself answers, 'The man shall be surely put to death.' That is also Rousseau's prescription for the punishment of the dissident citizen who is only an enemy of the state. Seldom has there been such a danger to freedom as is contained in this book.

The book contained an even greater danger to Rousseau's own freedom, after it was published, for in a chapter on Civil Religion, he developed the idea that the Christian religion was concerned only with the next world, not with this, which made it difficult for the citizen to know whether he should obey the magistrate or the priest. Christianity preaches only servitude and dependence, and invites tyranny. A single hypocrite, a Cromwell, would suffice to enslave the citizens. There must therefore be a civil religion, drawn up by the state, enjoining belief in a merciful God, a future life, blessings for the good and punishments for the evil.

As for the type of constitution to be adopted in the ideal state, democracy is applicable only to a population of gods. It is contrary to the nature of things for a majority to impose its will on a minority: there has never been a true democracy and never will be. These were strange words from the pen of a man who is generally taken to be the prophet of democracy. But the book also contained a passage to the effect that monarchical government must always be worse than republican, because in the latter the people elect only enlightened and capable men, whereas in the former those in power are mostly rascals and incompetent intriguers. Then, to cover himself in regard to the Prime Minister of France, the Duc de Choiseul, Rousseau added that when, by chance, a man born to govern takes charge of affairs in a monarchy, the effect is epoch-making. Choiseul failed to recognize himself in this passage.

The third of Rousseau's great trilogy of books was *Émile, ou de l'éducation*, also published in 1762. Since, by hypothesis, man was originally good before society corrupted him and made him evil, the child must obviously be good before society corrupts him. The first

A DEMOCRAT.

Caricature of a *sans culotte* of the French Revolution, regarded in England as the result of Rousseau's work

The Fête of the Supreme Being, revolutionary result of Rousseau's incursion into religion

ÉMILE,

OU

DE L'ÉDUCATION.

Par J. J. ROUSSEAU,
Citoyen de Genève.

Sanabilibus ægrotamus malis ; ipſaque nos in rectum
genitos natura, ſi emendari velimus, juvat.
Sen : de irâ. L. II. c. 13.

TOME PREMIER.

À AMSTERDAM,
Chez JEAN NÉAULME, Libraire.

M. DCC. LXII.
Avec Privilége de Noſſeign. les Etats de Hollande
& de Weſtfriſe.

task of education must be to protect the child from the evils of society. 'The childhood of children must be allowed to ripen.' As a self-taught man, Rousseau had nothing but scorn for colleges and universities. 'As the more men know the more they are mistaken, ignorance is the only way to avoid error.' Throughout the book there are echoes of his *Discours* on arts and sciences and on inequality, and of his *Contrat social*. 'If there is a miserable country in the world where everybody cannot make a living without committing a crime, it is not the criminal who should be hanged, but he who obliges him to commit it.' Rousseau also prophesies: 'We are approaching a state of crisis and a century of revolutions.' There follows a sombre note. 'I think it impossible that the great monarchies of Europe can last much longer.'

Émile revolves round a hypothetic child, Émile, who is 'educated' by a tutor, not a father. Bearing in mind what Rousseau had done to his own children, paternity to Émile was too painful. Émile's mother will breast-feed him herself, his tutor will take charge of his

Title-page of *Émile* and (*left*) frontispiece, showing Thetis dipping her son Achilles but holding his heel, where he remained vulnerable

(*Opposite*) Rousseau composing *Émile* in the Valley of Montmorency

(*Left*) Illustration from *Émile*, the gardener to Émile: 'Remember that I shall tear out your beans if you touch my melons'

(*Right*) Illustration from *Émile*, Sophie in the carpenter's shop; 'With her white frail hand, she pushes a plane on the plank'

instruction. He will be brought up in the country and inured to hardship, far from any products of society. His education will begin by being purely negative: no books of any kind, he must not learn to read. Instead, his senses must be sharpened. He will be taught nothing, but his curiosity will lead him to ask questions, and he will learn by the answers to these. Artificial faking of his situation by his tutor is permissible and desirable, to induce him to ask questions that he would not otherwise ask. He will learn by experience. For instance, Émile is encouraged to plant some beans in the gardener's garden. One day he is dismayed to find all the bean plants torn out. The gardener complains that he had planted melon seeds there and that his seedlings have been destroyed by the beans. In this way, Émile learns the meaning of property belonging to the first man to work on it. Émile will exercise his body and his senses so that he becomes stronger, more nimble, and more experienced than any other child of his age.

Next, after the age of twelve, comes positive education, in which Émile's intelligence will be fostered by meditation and reflection, but still without books. The rising and setting of the sun will introduce him to cosmology; his wanderings will teach him geography. He will be taught a handicraft and is apprenticed to a carpenter. At the age of fifteen, his tutor starts his instruction in 'natural religion', where Rousseau draws on his own experience from the time when the Abbé Gaime and the Abbé Gâtier were so helpful to him. On them is modelled the 'Profession of Faith of the Savoyard Vicar', which became the most controversial part of the book and was to involve Rousseau in serious trouble. Meanwhile, the tutor busies himself with the bride that Émile must have. She, Sophie (Mme d'Houdetot's name), will be brought up with an education aimed solely at her duties as wife and mother. A woman must never become learned, or a blue-stocking. Émile falls in love with Sophie, but the tutor insists that he must go away for two years, to make sure that he is master of his own passions. On his return he marries Sophie.

In this way the author who had sent his children to a foundling hospital, and never even set eyes on them, let alone educated them, prescribed an ideal programme of education. Everything in the book was fantastically impossible, but it had a great success, because he had written it, because the practice of hygiene that it advocated was useful and life in the country was becoming fashionable. In addition, problems of education were of growing interest.

The religious principles in the book consummated the rupture between Rousseau and his former *philosophe* friends. Although Rousseau's ideas are now regarded as progressive, they appeared unbearably reactionary to Voltaire and the *philosophes* who were campaigning against the Roman Church and the judicial murders that were being committed by Catholic zeal. Yet here was Rousseau, believing in God in his own way, and professing to be a Christian, albeit one that theologians could only condemn.

In his second *Discours* Rousseau set little store by medicine and doctors, but his urinary condition was now in urgent need of attention. He had developed a hernia which added to his trouble, because he had to press on his abdomen to empty his bladder. Crises of this disorder often coincided with fits of mental frenzy when he imagined that he was being cheated, tyrannized or deliberately misrepresented. This is not uncommon. At Mont-Louis, he made the acquaintance of two neighbours who, in spite of the disparity between their position and his, went to great trouble to help him. They were the Maréchal Duc de Luxembourg and his wife. The Duchesse de Luxembourg herself arranged for *Émile* to be published by a French publisher in Paris, because she thought that the Dutch publishers whom Rousseau had hitherto employed did not give him good enough terms. He suddenly gave way to a pathological outburst of terror, because there were delays in printing. His

The Maréchal Duc de Luxembourg, benefactor and protector of Rousseau

nightmare was that the manuscript of *Émile* had got into the hands of Jesuits who would alter his text and, substituting another, would present to posterity under his name views that were the reverse of his own. Despairing of recognition by his contemporaries, he became all the more frenzied in his anxiety that he should shine in the eyes of posterity which, he was convinced, 'would love him'.

There was, of course, no basis for this mental storm, but it coincided with the fear that he was suffering from a stone in his bladder and that he would soon undergo agonies. He thought that his days were numbered and made two requests to the Duchesse de Luxembourg: to care for Thérèse when he had gone, and to try to trace the eldest of the children he had abandoned to the foundling hospital. The Duc de Luxembourg went to the trouble of finding the most capable surgeon, a urologist called Jean Baseilhac, better known as Frère Côme. Luxembourg brought him to Rousseau's house in person, and stayed in the room for two hours while the surgeon performed the delicate operation of passing a long fine probe all the way into Rousseau's bladder. He was able to reassure Rousseau that he had no stone in his bladder, and that, although his prostate was enlarged, he would live a long life, but suffer much pain. Some weeks later, a probe broke in his urethra and could not be extracted, which made his trouble worse, but it passed out some months later. It was in order to facilitate these operations that Rousseau got an Armenian tailor at Montmorency to make him a dress, with a furry hat and a long coat or kaftan, but no breeches.

During this period a storm was brewing in Paris, because it was obviously dangerous for a Calvinist to introduce into France such books as the *Contrat social* and *Émile* in the year 1762. Rousseau had always thought that he was safe from prosecution because he was Swiss and his books were printed in Holland and did not have to be submitted to French censorship. He assumed that the censor, his friend M. de Malesherbes, could be relied on to turn a blind eye. But Rousseau had tempted providence too far. On 8 June 1762 the Prince de Conti, who had a soft spot for him, sent a message to the Luxembourgs to say that on the following day the Parlement of Paris was going to issue a warrant for the burning of *Émile* by the common executioner and the arrest of Rousseau. In the middle of the night the Duchesse sent a servant to Rousseau's house to warn him and to urge him to leave France immediately. On 9 June he left in a cabriolet, making for the Swiss frontier, and when he reached it, he got out and kissed the soil of a land of freedom, as he thought. On 14 June he arrived at the house of his old friend Daniel Roguin, at Yverdon.

Luckily, Rousseau had avoided going to Geneva, where the French Ambassador was very powerful. On 19 June the government of Geneva issued a warrant for the burning of *Émile* and the

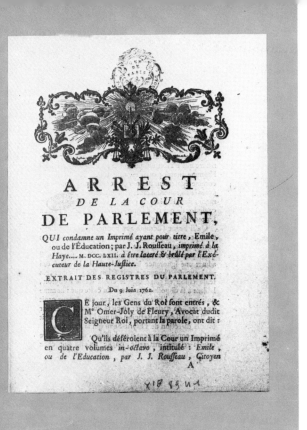

Contrat social, and for Rousseau's arrest. Soon afterwards the government of Berne ordered Rousseau to leave its territory, for Yverdon, in the Pays de Vaud, had been under Bernese sovereignty since 1536 when Berne conquered it from Savoy. Roguin's niece, Mme Boy de la Tour, owned a little house at Môtiers-Travers, in the neighbouring principality of Neuchâtel, and placed it at Rousseau's disposal.

The sovereign of Neuchâtel was Frederick the Great, king of Prussia, and the governor was George Keith, Earl Marischal of Scotland, always known locally as 'milord maréchal'. He had been attainted in Great Britain for the part he played in the Jacobite Rebellion of 1715. His residence was the Château de Colombier, near Neuchâtel, where he welcomed Rousseau. They became close friends, and Keith obtained for Rousseau the sovereign's permission to reside in the principality and, later, letters of naturalization. At last Rousseau was in a situation after his own heart, living in a beautiful country, in the valley of the Areuse, surrounded by the hills of the Jura range, among simple peasants, but also enjoying the friendship of the governor and local notabilities. Thérèse arrived on 20 July and there seemed nothing to prevent Rousseau from living the life of his dreams indefinitely.

Country, simplicity and freedom – and to these was shortly to be added botany, to the pleasures of which he was introduced by Jean-Antoine d'Ivernois. With a donkey carrying blankets and provisions, and his friends, especially Pierre-Alexandre du Peyrou and Jean-Jacques de Luze, Rousseau made one excursion after another to the different valleys, slopes and crests of the Jura, sleeping in hay-barns, picnicking in the open, collecting and identifying plants, and comparing those found by his companions, all as happy as sandboys. At home, Rousseau baked his own bread, a return to primitive conditions of life, but he paid a fee to the village oven-keeper for this privilege.

The river Doubs where it expands into the Lac des Brenets, on which Rousseau sailed and on the banks of which he botanized, near Môtiers-Travers

(*Above*) Môtiers-Travers, by the river Areuse in the Val de Travers, showing Rousseau's house on the right, in the principality of Neuchâtel

(*Left*) The Falls of the Doubs, one of the goals for Rousseau's excursions from Môtiers-Travers

Christophe de Beaumont, Archbishop of Paris, author of the Pastoral Letter ('Mandement') attacking Rousseau and his *Émile*, in answer to which Rousseau wrote his *Lettre à Christophe de Beaumont* in which he claimed that an enlightened government would erect statues to the author of *Émile*

Unfortunately, Rousseau's past could not help overtaking him, and he brought down on himself one load of trouble after another. The warrant for his arrest in Paris was followed by a Pastoral Letter from the Archbishop of Paris, Christophe de Beaumont, condemning *Émile*. It was a declaration of anathema on a grand scale. 'Saint Paul predicted, dearly beloved Brethren, that dangerous days would come when there would be men infatuated with themselves, proud, overbearing, blasphemers, impious, calumniators, inflated with conceit, seeking voluptuousness instead of God; men of corrupt minds and perverted faith.'

This Pastoral Letter rankled with Rousseau as much as the warrant for his arrest issued by the Parlement of Paris. He decided to reply to the Archbishop in a book, *Lettre à Christophe de Beaumont*. It was a new conflict between David and Goliath: the powerless little Protestant layman fighting the powerful Catholic Archbishop. Rousseau began with a lie, when he claimed that he had become an author and been thrown into celebrity in spite of himself.

JEAN JAQUES ROUSSEAU,

CITOYEN DE GENÈVE,

A

CHRISTOPHE DE BEAUMONT,

*Archevêque de Paris, Duc de St. Cloud,
Pair de France, Commandeur de
l'Ordre du St. Esprit, Proviseur
de Sorbonne, &c.*

Da veniam si quid liberius dixi, non ad con-
tumeliam tuam, sed ad defensionem meam.
Præsumsi enim de gravitate & prudentiâ tuâ,
quia potes considerare quantam mihi res-
pondendi necessitatem imposueris.
Aug. Epist. 238 ad Pascent.

A AMSTERDAM,
Chez MARC MICHEL REY,
MDCCLXIII.

He was fishing for pity, but then proceeded to refute the Arch-bishop's accusations point by point. After much skilful argument, he ended in heroic style:

My Lord, you have insulted me publicly, and I have just proved to you that you have calumniated me. If you were a private person like me, and I were able to summon you to appear before an impartial tribunal, you with your Pastoral Letter and I with my *Émile*, you would surely be found guilty and condemned to make me reparation as public as your libel. But you occupy a rank where you are absolved from the duty of acting with justice, and I am nothing. Nevertheless, you, Prelate, appointed to teach others their duty, you know your own in such a case. As for me, I have done mine. I have no more to say to you, and I hold my peace.

In this combative book, Rousseau insisted on his being a Christian, but a Christian who would have nothing to do with St Paul's doctrine of original sin, or with grace, fear or the mystery of pre-destination. While obviously unacceptable to Roman Catholics, this view was no more palatable to Calvinists. The degree of his self-assurance can be measured from the following passage in this

(*Left*) Illustration from *Émile* showing the Savoyard Vicar saying to Émile: 'I believe that the world is governed by a powerful and wise will'

(*Right*) Title-page of Rousseau's *Lettre à Christophe de Beaumont*

book: 'Yes, I am not afraid of saying it; if in Europe there was a single enlightened government, whose views were really useful and sane, it would have given public honours to the author of *Émile* and erected statues to him.'

The action of the government of Geneva rankled with him even more. On 21 January 1761 it had forbidden lending libraries to handle *La nouvelle Héloïse*. Now he was incensed at what he considered to be the illegal condemnation of *Émile* and the *Contrat social*, because questions of theological orthodoxy were the province of the consistory court of pastors, not of the government. Further, no warrant could legally be issued for the arrest of an author unless he was given a hearing. His friends in Geneva made representations to the government about the irregularity of its treatment of Rousseau and for this reason these friends became known as 'représentants', while those who supported the government in rejecting the representations were known as 'négatifs'. In this way, Rousseau became the subject of a political split in the republic. As the government had taken the further step of prohibiting the reprinting of Rousseau's *Lettre à Christophe de Beaumont* in Geneva, and he considered that the 'représentants' had not been sufficiently active in vindicating him, he decided to take a drastic and dramatic step. On 12 May 1763 he renounced his citizenship of Geneva and was now a stateless person.

Rousseau's renunciation made the strife between the parties in the city even more bitter. The public prosecutor of Geneva, Jean-Robert Tronchin, wrote a book, *Lettres écrites de la campagne*, to justify the actions of the government. Rousseau replied with his *Lettres écrites de la montagne*, which fairly set the cat among the pigeons in Geneva, on theological as well as political grounds. In his *Lettre à Christophe de Beaumont* he had purposely exaggerated his defence of Protestant principles, in the hope that this would ingratiate him with the authorities in Geneva. Now he leant over to the Catholic side, in case he should again live in France.

The *Lettres écrites de la montagne* were a tactical mistake for two reasons. Firstly, having renounced his citizenship of Geneva, Rousseau had lost his right to intervene or to criticize its government or its religion. Secondly, he left his vulnerable flank open to Voltaire who had been waiting for Rousseau to overreach himself. Voltaire now had a splendid opportunity to hit Rousseau where it would hurt him most. Pretending to be a citizen of Geneva, Voltaire published an anonymous pamphlet called *Le sentiment des citoyens,* in which the author asks, Who is this man who thinks that statues ought to be erected to him, and with the same humility compares his life with that of Jesus, who outrages the Christian religion and the Reformation, and insults our governors and pastors? Is it a learned man, arguing against other learned men? No, it is a pox-

Rousseau's motto *Vitam impendere vero* ('to submit one's life to the truth') from the title-page of his *Lettres écrites de la montagne*, 1764. He had a seal made of it and used it for the rest of his life

Fanciful representation of Rousseau and Voltaire fighting. They never met, but after the anonymous publication of Voltaire's *Le sentiment des citoyens* and other attacks on Rousseau when he was in England, the enmity between them was public knowledge

marked wretch of a clown who drags after him from village to village and from mountain to mountain, a trollop whose mother he has killed and whose children, born to him, he has exposed at the door of a foundling hospital.

The gloves were now off, but the awful secret was out. Rousseau's conscience was dreadfully pricked, but the step that he now took did nothing to ease it. He sent Voltaire's pamphlet to Paris to be reprinted with notes of his own, refuting the allegations it contained. He gave the names of doctors who could give evidence that he had never suffered from venereal disease (which was true). He asserted that Mme Levasseur was living and in good health (which was also true); and that he had never exposed any children at the door of a foundling hospital (which was true in letter but not in spirit, for the children had been carried safely inside the hospital by the midwife). He had lied, not only to the world but to himself. This uneasy conscience made him think of writing his *Confessions*. He had recently had a seal made for himself, bearing the inscription *vitam impendere vero* ('to submit one's life to the truth'). With all this professed devotion to truth, he must come clean in the end.

Rousseau's troubles did not cease with these vexations on a background of politics: theology took over. Catholic criticisms of his religious views, as expressed by the Savoyard Vicar, were already contained in the Archbishop's Pastoral Letter. Now it was the turn of Protestants to attack him. When he first arrived at Môtiers-Travers, the pastor, Frédéric-Guillaume de Montmollin, not a little proud of having such a celebrity in his parish, heard his profession of faith and admitted him to communion. At Geneva, however, headquarters of Calvinist orthodoxy, there was a pastor, Jean Sarasin, very zealous in defence of the faith of the Reformation, who picked out all the unacceptable and unorthodox pronounce-ments in Rousseau's *Émile*, *Contrat social*, and *Lettres écrites de la montagne*, and drew them to the attention of the pastor of Môtiers-Travers.

Rousseau's unorthodoxy can be treated under six heads. First, the doubt whether Rousseau believed in the necessity of the Christian revelation for access to God, for he was always harping on 'natural religion', based on nature and man's own conscience.

Next came the multiplicity of religions on earth. Two-thirds of the human race are neither Jews, nor Muslims, nor Christians. Rousseau argued that if there is only one true religion, it is necessary to study them all. Are the miracles sufficient historical proof of Christianity? After proving the doctrine by the miracles, it is necessary to prove the miracles by the doctrine. Rousseau preferred to believe in spite of the miracles.

This led on to Rousseau's questioning the historical credibility of the Gospels. God has spoken, but to whom? To men – and it is men who say what God has said. Who wrote the Gospels? Men. Who attest the truth of the miracles? Men. 'I should have preferred to hear God myself,' said Rousseau: 'What a lot of men between me and God.'

Then there was the question of the origin of morals. For Rousseau, this was 'Conscience, divine instinct, eternal heavenly voice, sure guide of the ignorant and of the learned, the enslaved and the free; infallible judge of good and evil.' This was quite insufficient for priests and pastors, who required a Day of Judgment, rewards and pains after death, to keep their flocks on the straight and narrow path. Even less acceptable was Rousseau's argument that, as God was inexhaustible goodness, it was improper to pray to him for anything that he had already given.

A very touchy point was the definition of the Reformation as professed by the Calvinist Church. Rousseau claimed that, being reformed, the Church of Geneva had no precise profession of faith since it was based on the free interpretation of the Scriptures, on the authority of reason in matters of faith, on evangelical tolerance, and on obedience to the law. This also was clearly unacceptable.

Finally, there was Rousseau's assertion in the *Contrat social*, that Christianity had no connection with the body politic but was concerned only with the world of the spirit, which was why there must be a civil religion, drawn up by the state, to ensure that every citizen shall love his duties on earth.

Rousseau's honeymoon period at Môtiers-Travers was drawing to its close. His health continued to trouble him, and he took to hewing wood to make himself sweat, and thus reduce the fluid input to his bladder. Now even worse troubles were about to overtake him. Montmollin at last realized that he had been hasty and negligent in admitting Rousseau to the fold. He summoned Rousseau to a meeting to answer questions on his faith. Rousseau refused to appear. The controversy reached the ears of Frederick the Great, who issued orders for Rousseau to be withdrawn from the competence of the consistory of pastors, but to no avail. Montmollin preached a sermon against the unrighteous, in which the whole parish recognized Rousseau, and on 6 September 1765, stones were thrown at his house. He left for Neuchâtel on the 8th, and on the 12th he took refuge on the Île Saint-Pierre, a tiny island in the Lake of Bienne, on which there was only one house, belonging to the receiver of Berne, with whom he lodged.

The Île Saint-Pierre in the Lake of Bienne seen from the northern shore near La Neuveville. Rousseau took refuge there after stones were thrown at his house at Môtiers-Travers

(*Above*) The house of the receiver of Berne in which Rousseau stayed, on the Île Saint-Pierre, in September 1765

(*Right*) The living room in the receiver's house on the Île Saint-Pierre

(*Above*) Rousseau, Thérèse, his dog Sultan, the receiver's wife and sister, taking rabbits to populate a tiny island near the Île Saint-Pierre

(*Left*) Fanciful engraving of Rousseau's bedroom on the Île Saint-Pierre, with visitors coming in while Rousseau disappears through a trapdoor on the right

(*Left*) Rockhall, the house at Bienne belonging to Rodolphe Vautravers, a Swiss naturalized English, who invited Rousseau to stay after he had been expelled from the Île Saint-Pierre

(*Right*) William Kenrick, who translated Rousseau's important books into English and drew him to the attention of English readers. With a party of Scotsmen, Kenrick visited Rousseau at Môtiers-Travers in 1765

For as long as he was there, he lived an idyllic existence, isolated from the world, collecting plants and drifting about in a little boat on the lake, without any cares. He contemplated compiling a flora of the island. But the island belonged to Berne, whose government was no more amicably disposed to his books than those of Paris or Geneva. Casanova once asked the great Bernese polymath Albrecht von Haller what he thought of *La nouvelle Héloïse*. 'It is the worst of novels', Haller replied, 'because it is the most eloquent.' The government of Berne ordered Rousseau to leave the Île Saint-Pierre. In desperation he petitioned Their Excellencies of Berne to put him in prison wherever they chose, and promised never to write anything more. But it was to no avail, and on 25 October 1765 he left and went to Bienne, a little town which formed part of the bishopric of Basle. A Swiss who had been naturalized English, Rodolphe Vautravers, lived there in a fine house, Rockhall, and he invited Rousseau to stay.

Rousseau's name was known in Britain from the time his two *Discours* were translated into English. But it was his three great books, translated by William Kenrick, that brought him fame there. The condemnation of *Émile* and the *Contrat social* in Paris and Geneva, and also in The Hague, whetted British appetites for their translations. When Rousseau took refuge at Môtiers-Travers, his name and fame were already well known to British travellers and many came to visit him.

When Edward Gibbon returned to Lausanne in 1763, he had already broken off his engagement to Suzanne Curchod, who was earning her living as nursemaid in the family of Rousseau's friend Paul Moultou, pastor of Geneva. Greatly distressed by Gibbon's

(*Left*) Paul Moultou, pastor of Geneva, Rousseau's most steadfast friend

(*Right*) Thomas Hollis, the English republican, who advised Rousseau to visit England but not to stay there

hardness of heart, Moultou begged Rousseau to intercede with Gibbon for Suzanne. Rousseau had another look at Gibbon's book, *Essai sur l'étude de la littérature,* and replied that as Mr Gibbon was not the man for him, he did not believe that he could be the man for Mlle Curchod.

In the same year, Peter Beckford, the expert on fox-hunting, came to see Rousseau, who told him that he had not accepted invitations to take refuge in England only because of his gratitude to his French benefactors, and England was at war with France. Rousseau went on to tell him, 'I hate books: they only teach you to speak about what you don't know.'

In May 1764, Daniel Malthus, father of the economist, came to visit Rousseau and laid the foundations of further connections with him in England when he invited Rousseau to Surrey. But the star turn of the year was the buffoon James Boswell. Shortly before his arrival, Rousseau had in September 1764 received an invitation on behalf of Pasquale di Paoli to draft a political constitution for Corsica. Under Paoli's leadership, Corsica had shaken off the yoke of its sovereign, the Republic of Genoa. In the *Contrat social,* Rousseau had said that Corsica was the only country left in Europe capable of sound legislation, and Boswell told him that he was going to Corsica. He even offered to be Rousseau's ambassador there. In his Journal, Boswell described Thérèse as a 'little lively French girl'.

There had been much talk of Rousseau going to England, and in May 1765, Vautravers received a letter from Thomas Hollis, the republican evangelical rationalist, containing the following reference to Rousseau:

James Boswell dressed as a Corsican Chief, as he appeared at Shakespeare's jubilee in 1769

If the excellent Rousseau should choose to see England as a visitor, he would benefit his health by it, it is probable, and be variously entertained by the journey; and he would, I am confident, be well received here and universally respected. But, bad as he has been at his time of life and as we are all of us under the force of certain habits, to settle here is not the country for him. As for quiet, who sees not the Storm, that is gathering to burst on us? The Idea of giving up all literature, and parting with all his books, is that of an over-worked ill-treated man, and the accomplished, active and beneficent Rousseau, after relaxation, which he should take, will himself be the foremost to oppugn to it.

Had Rousseau taken this advice it would have saved him many vexations. The 'Storm' was what Hollis foresaw would be the result of the Stamp Act in the American colonies.

At Bienne, Rousseau was uncertain whether to remain for the winter or to go. An Englishman turned up who decided him: Dr John Turton, afterwards physician in ordinary to George III, had come from Berlin with an invitation from Marischal Keith for Rousseau to take refuge there. Rousseau decided to leave Switzerland, but not to go to Berlin. Instead he was going to take advantage of David Hume's invitation to England. Leaving Thérèse on the Île Saint-Pierre, Rousseau left Bienne on 29 October 1765, and on 2 November arrived at Strasbourg. It was a risky thing for him to enter France where the warrant for his arrest was still valid, but he was received with enthusiasm and his opera *Le Devin du village* was performed in his honour. He received an invitation from the Cossack hetman of the Ukraine, Cyril Razoumovsky, to take refuge in Russia but refused it. On 9 December he left Strasbourg and arrived in Paris on the 16th. The Prince de Conti, Grand Prior of the Order of the Knights Hospitaller in France, invited

Dr John Turton, who met Rousseau at Bienne and gave him Marischal Keith's invitation to go to Berlin

Dover, where Rousseau landed in England with David Hume on 11 January 1766

him to stay in the palace of Le Temple. Rousseau's *Les Muses galantes* was performed, and he was lionized.

On 4 January 1766, in company with David Hume and Jean-Jacques de Luze, Rousseau set off for London. They put up for the night successively at Senlis, Roye, Arras and Aire, and reached Calais on 8 January. At midday on the 11th they landed at Dover after a bad night crossing. Spending a night each at Canterbury and Dartford, they reached London on Monday, 13 January, and stayed at a house in Buckingham Street, Strand.

Rousseau's arrival had been eagerly awaited. On 10 January William Rouet, a Scotsman then in London, wrote to his friend Baron William Mure of Caldwell, to say that the travellers were expected daily. In his next letter, dated 16 January, Rouet described Hume as very busy trying to find a place for Rousseau in the country. The newspapers were all agog. *The Gazetteer and New Daily Advertizer* for 20 January wrote: 'The ingenious Mr Rousseau arrived in town last Monday in company with David Hume Esq. It was a mistake that Mr Rousseau had gone to Putney; he is in Buckingham Street in the Strand. We hear that this learned citizen of Geneva, and writer of several spirited works, is so desirous of retirement, that he has prevailed on his friends here, that he may go down to Radnorshire in Wales, to board and lodge with a farmer who lives in a mansion-house of a worthy gentleman of that county.' This gentleman was Chase Price of Knighton, M.P. for Leominster and later for Radnorshire, Receiver of Customs fines.

Hume had indeed been busy, as Rouet said. On 17 January, Hume and Rousseau inspected the house of a French gardener at Fulham, but it had to let only one room with two beds, one of them occupied by a sick person. A Mr Townsend offered accommodation in his house near London, but that did not suit because Rousseau insisted that Thérèse must take her meals with the family. As early as 1762 when Rousseau fled from France, Hans Stanley of Paultons (grandson of Sir Hans Sloane) had offered Rousseau a house on the Isle of Wight and, now that Stanley had become Constable of Carisbrooke Castle and Governor of the Isle of Wight, he renewed the offer. Rousseau declined it because the country was described as not wooded enough for his liking, it was exposed to high winds, it contained too many inhabitants and the price of necessities was reputed to be as high as in London.

There were too many people in Buckingham Street to please Rousseau, for it was thronged with visitors, curious to see the lion, and Hume found himself turned into a showman. The Duke of York, Lord Nuneham, the Hereditary Prince of Brunswick, Colonel Webb and the Rev. Richard Penneck, rector of Abinger and Keeper of the Reading Room of the British Museum, were among the crowd.

No. 10 Buckingham Street, Strand, where Rousseau stayed from 13 to 31 January 1766 and streams of visitors called on him

David Hume, Rousseau's first host in England, soon to become his worst enemy

Monaughty, the house in Radnorshire belonging to Chase Price who offered Rousseau lodgings in it

Before long, Hume discovered that his magnanimity in offering to find shelter for Rousseau in England had not taken account of his ward's impossibly difficult character. Lord Charlemont throws light on this:

When Hume and Rousseau arrived from France, happening to meet with Hume in the Park, I wished him joy of his pleasing connection, and particularly hinted that I was convinced he must be perfectly happy in his new friend, as their sentiments were, I believed, nearly similar. 'Why no, man', said he, 'you are mistaken. Rousseau is not what you think him; he has a hankering after the Bible, and indeed is little better than a Christian in a way of his own.' Excess of vanity was the madness of Rousseau. When he first arrived in London he and his Armenian dress were followed by crowds, and as long as this species of admiration lasted, he was contented and happy.

On 18 January, Hume learnt that Chase Price was prepared to let Rousseau have a lodging in his house, Monaughty, an old sixteenth-century monastery building near Presteigne in Radnorshire, where one of his farmers lived. On 20 January Price called on Rousseau and promised to write that day to his farmer and instruct him to get everything ready. Rousseau would pay £30 a year for his and Thérèse's board and lodging. Everything seemed to be settled.

On Thursday, 23 January, a royal performance was given at Drury Lane Theatre. George III and Queen Charlotte were eager to see the new visitor to England; but Hume had the greatest difficulty in making Rousseau come, because he was afraid that in his absence his dog Sultan would escape. Hume shut the door with

Sultan inside, took the key away, and forced Rousseau to come with him. *The London Evening Post* for 23–25 January 1766 printed the following report on the performance. 'Thursday, just as their Majesties came into Drury Lane theatre to see the tragedy of Zara, the celebrated John James Rousseau made his appearance in the upper box, over the stage box, fronting their Majesties. He was dressed in a foreign dress and accompanied by Mr Hume. The crowd was so great at getting into the theatre, that a great number of Gentlemen lost their hats and wigs, and Ladies their cloaks, &c. There was a great disturbance in the Upper Gallery at the above theatre, which prevented Mrs Yates and Miss Plym from going on, just as they had opened the piece.' After the performance, as Joseph Cradock the author wrote, 'the celebrated foreigner was treated with a most elegant supper at Mr Garrick's house in the Adelphi; and many of the first literary characters were invited to give him the meeting.'

There was nothing to do but wait for Monaughty to be ready. Rousseau, weary of London, went on 31 January to Chiswick, to lodge with a grocer named Pulleyn. Hume returned to his old lodgings in Lisle Street. On 13 February, Thérèse arrived and went to Chiswick. Rousseau had suggested that she might come from the Île Saint-Pierre by the boat which left Yverdon, sailed through the lakes of Neuchâtel and Bienne, down the rivers Aar and Rhine, across the sea and up the Thames to London. But Thérèse came a very different way. She went to Paris and stayed in the house of

David Garrick and Miss Younge acting in *Zara*, the play seen by Rousseau at Drury Lane

Chiswick. The grocer Pulleyn's house, where Rousseau stayed, was one of those by the river side

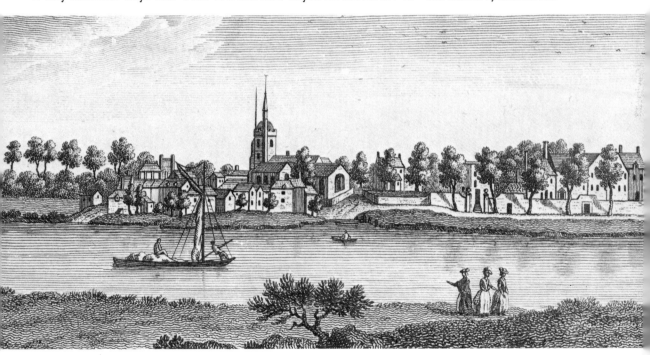

James Boswell, who escorted Thérèse from Paris and brought her to Rousseau at Chiswick

Horace Walpole, afterwards 4th Earl of Orford, author of the hoax letter to Rousseau from the King of Prussia

the Duchesse de Luxembourg, where Boswell called on her. She was anxious about the journey to London and suggested that she and Boswell should travel together. They left Paris on 31 January 1766. Boswell was in bad spirits because he had just learnt that his mother had died. But they revived after the first night of the journey and, as he and Thérèse then shared the same bed, they mated thirteen times, many of these under the 'tuition' of Thérèse, who told Boswell that he was 'vigorous' but had no 'art'. Boswell took her to Rousseau at Chiswick on 13 February. Subsequently, Rousseau wrote to Boswell urging him to look after his health and to be bled frequently.

Events soon became complicated as a result of a cruel hoax by Horace Walpole, who was then in Paris. He composed a bogus letter from Frederick the Great to Rousseau, written in French. The English translation ran:

My dear Jean-Jacques, You have renounced Geneva, your native soil. You have been driven from Switzerland, a country of which you have made such boast in your writings. In France you are outlawed: come then to me. I admire your talents, and amuse myself with your reveries; on which however, by the way, you bestow too much time and attention. It is high time to grow prudent and happy: you have made yourself sufficiently talked of for singularities little becoming a truly great man: show your enemies that you have sometimes common sense: this will vex them without hurting you. My dominions afford you a peaceful retreat: I am desirous to do you good, and will do it, if you can but think it such. But if you are determined to refuse my assistance, you may expect that I shall not say a word about it to anyone. If you persist in perplexing your brains to find new misfortunes, chuse such as you like best; I am a King and can make you as miserable as you can wish: at the same time I will engage to do that which your enemies never will, I will cease to persecute you, when you are no longer vain of persecution. Your sincere friend, Frederick.

The laugh was going round Paris even before Rousseau's departure, but he got to hear of it in London and unfortunately became suspicious that Hume had had something to do with it.

A new calamity which Hume reported on 16 February was that the dog, Sultan, had got lost, and he put notices in the newspapers. Samuel Rogers's *Table-Talk* described the sequel: 'While Rousseau was lodging in Chiswick Terrace, Fitzpatrick called upon him one day, and was not long in the room when David Hume entered. Rousseau had lost a favourite dog; and Hume, having exerted himself to recover it, now brought it back to its master, who thanked him with expressions of the most fervent gratitude, and shed tears of joy over the animal.'

But Sultan got lost again. On 1 March, Rousseau went to sit to Allan Ramsay in Harley Street for his portrait, at Hume's request. On the walk back to Chiswick, Sultan disappeared. Lord Strafford, who had recently called on Rousseau, promised to put an advertisement in the newspapers, and it appeared in *The Public*

(*Left*) Part of Rocque's Map of Surrey, showing the sites of Munday House where Rousseau stayed with Colonel Charles Webb, Sir John Evelyn's Wotton Place, and Daniel Malthus's The Rookery

(*Right*) Mundies Farm in 1955. Its condition in 1766 when Rousseau stayed with Colonel Webb is difficult to determine because its outhouses were used to store munitions which blew up in a forest fire in 1942

Advertiser for Tuesday, 4 March 1766: 'Lost, last Saturday evening, between Kensington and Chiswick, a small brown Dog, with short Ears, and a short curled Tail. Whoever brings him to Mr Pulleyn's Grocer, by the River's side, Chiswick, shall have Five shillings reward. No greater Reward will be offered.' Sultan returned on his own.

A piece of good news was that on 2 March Rousseau learnt that his luggage, feared to have been lost, had been found in the Customs. But all this time the house in Wales hung fire. Hume asked Daniel Malthus, Rousseau's friend who lived at The Rookery, Dorking, and the Rev. Richard Penneck of Abinger if they knew of a house that Rousseau might take in their neighbourhood. There came an answer from Colonel Charles Webb, recommended by Malthus. Colonel Charles Webb lived at Munday House, about half a mile south of Sir John Evelyn's Wotton Place. Munday House can be pin-pointed on John Rocque's Map of Surrey of 1768, in that part of Surrey known as 'Little Switzerland'.

About 7 March 1766, Rousseau with Thérèse and Hume set off for Surrey and spent two nights in Colonel Webb's house. Rousseau appeared to be enchanted with the natural beauties and the solitude of the place, and Hume entered into negotiations with a view to 'making an establishment' for Rousseau there. When inspected in 1955, Mundies Farm (as it was then called) was a poorly restored cottage, converted into two dwellings with low ceilings and small rooms. It is difficult to judge of its state when

The Rookery near Dorking, home of Daniel Malthus who tried unsuccessfully to get Rousseau to stay with him in March 1766. A few days previously, his son Thomas Robert Malthus, afterwards author of the *Essay on the Principle of Population*, was born in this house

Rousseau stayed there, because of an accident in the Second World War. Its outhouses, well hidden by trees, were used by the army for the storage of munitions, but they blew up in a forest fire in 1942.

Rousseau decided against Colonel Webb's house, and the party visited two other houses mentioned by Malthus, but they did not suit either. On the return journey to London, Malthus tried to get Rousseau to spend the night in his own house, The Rookery. A few days previously, Thomas Robert Malthus, the future author of the *Essay on the Principle of Population*, had been born in that house; but Rousseau preferred to continue his journey and returned to Chiswick about 9 March.

A curious legend has been built up into folklore about Rousseau's visit to Wotton and Abinger which was made to last for several days, during which Rousseau was supposed to have made a habit of walking in one of the alleys of the Park of Wotton Place. A statue of a female figure was erected in about 1880 in 'Rousseau's Walk' to commemorate this. There is no truth in this at all, but the whole legend has been incorporated as fact in the *Victoria County History of Surrey*.

(*Left*) Wotton Place, Surrey, seat of Sir John Evelyn. Rousseau's stay of two nights at Colonel Webb's house, Mundies, and his looking at houses at Wotton and Abinger, gave rise to a legend that he had spent several days at Wotton and that he constantly walked in an alley of the park at Wotton Place. (*Below*) the statue erected by W. J. Evelyn about 1880 in the park at Wotton Place to commemorate 'Rousseau's Walk': entirely bogus

The house in Wales was still not ready, but Rousseau learnt that Richard Davenport, a wealthy philanthropist, was ready to put at Rousseau's immediate disposal his splendid mansion of Wootton Hall, in Staffordshire, near Ashbourne in Derbyshire. Rousseau accepted, provided that Davenport agreed he should receive £30 a year for Rousseau's and Thérèse's board and lodging. As the house was ready, servants and all, Rousseau wrote to Price on 15 March to explain why he had decided to go to Staffordshire.

From Chiswick, on 18 March, Rousseau and Thérèse came to London to lodge with Hume in Lisle Street, in order to take the chaise to Wootton Hall. It was an unfortunate meeting. Hume's landlady disapproved of the visitors, and Thérèse was put into a room in an attic which Rousseau described as 'a kennel'. A letter arrived for Rousseau, whose correspondence came and went through Hume who paid the costs of postage. Rousseau sat down to answer it then and there, but suspected that Hume was hanging around his shoulders to read what he had written. This suspicion became worse when Hume insisted that his footman should take it to the post office, rather than the footman of Lord Nuneham who

(*Left*) Wootton Hall, Staffordshire, which Richard Davenport placed at Rousseau's disposal for £30 a year, board and lodging with servants for him and Thérèse. It has since been pulled down

(*Right*) Richard Davenport (1705–71), owner of Wootton Hall, benefactor and protector of Rousseau for whom he obtained a pension of £100 from the King

had come to call and offered to take it. The evening ended in a pathetic scene, with Rousseau bursting into tears on Hume's knees, uncertain whether his host was a traitor or himself a villain.

Further trouble arose over the journey by chaise from London to Wootton Hall, which they reached on 22 March. Davenport had let Rousseau understand that he had found a return chaise, so that the expense of Rousseau's journey would be small. This subterfuge was exposed when Rousseau saw the driver turn round and return to London. He made bitter reproaches at this practice of giving him charity by deception. It went straight against his principle that friendship was incompatible with gratitude, a principle by which he defended his unconditional independence. But all this was soon overtaken by far more serious trouble.

The London newspapers had begun by giving Rousseau a wel/come, but the mood soon changed. On 1 April 1766, *The Saint James's Chronicle* published the hoax *Letter from the King of Prussia* in English and in French. Rousseau was unwise enough to get a protest published in the same paper on 8 April. There was then a spate of ironical letters ragging Rousseau, and as he was utterly devoid of any sense of humour, he took all this as a personal affront. His morbid sensitivity was outraged; but worst of all was the publication in English of the anonymous letter from Voltaire to 'J./J. Pansophe', in which Rousseau's leg was pulled mercilessly. This he thought was open hostility.

General Henry Seymour Conway, Secretary of State, who obtained the King's consent to a pension for Rousseau. Later, in a demented state, Rousseau implored Conway to be allowed to leave England unmolested

Even before landing in England, Hume had asked Rousseau if he would accept a pension from George III, and as Rousseau agreed Hume set the ball rolling. On 2 May 1766, General Henry Seymour Conway, the Secretary of State, saw the King who agreed to a pension of £100 a year for Rousseau, but it must be kept secret. Delighted 'in having contributed to procure for one of his distinguish'd genius and merit these marks of favour and protection which will do honour to this country, and in a particular manner to the Royal hand from which this bounty flows', Conway wrote to Hume, who enclosed Conway's letter with his own to Rousseau. To this Hume received no answer, but on 12 May, Rousseau replied direct to Conway, saying how much he regretted not being able at that moment to accept the King's pension; he was too upset. Neither Conway nor Hume could make head or tail of Rousseau's behaviour, and Hume repeatedly pressed Rousseau for an explanation. Hume thought it possible that it was the condition of secrecy that made Rousseau refuse and that he would accept at once if it was made public. At the same time, Hume wrote to Davenport, who lived near Wootton Hall and often visited Rousseau, to ask if he could understand what was happening. The confusion grew when Davenport replied that, far from being upset or in ill health, Rousseau was very well and in good spirits. Most incomprehensible of all, Rousseau denied to Davenport that he had ever refused the pension from the King, of whom he spoke with the utmost respect.

King George III, who was deeply interested in Rousseau and granted him a pension which Rousseau afterwards renounced

85

Anne-Robert-Jacques Turgot, Baron de l'Aulne (1727–81), French statesman. When Rousseau returned to France, where a warrant was open for his arrest, it was to Turgot that Hume wrote urging him to use his best endeavours with Louis XV and the Duc de Choiseul to give Rousseau protection

Some of Hume's friends, including Anne-Robert-Jacques Turgot, the French statesman, and Adam Smith the economist, had seen the true meaning of Rousseau's letter to Conway; it did not mean that Rousseau refused to receive a pension from the King, but that Rousseau refused to receive it at the hands of Hume who, he had now convinced himself, was in league with Voltaire, d'Alembert, Diderot and his other enemies, to disgrace him.

There followed Rousseau's terrible letter to Hume of 10 July 1766, in which all his suspicions of Hume's treacherous behaviour were enumerated.

First, on the journey from Paris, at Senlis, Hume had said in his sleep, 'I have got Jean-Jacques Rousseau.' Next there was the letter that Hume tried to read over Rousseau's shoulder and insisted on posting. There was another letter to Rousseau which seemed to him to have been opened and resealed, which convinced him that Hume was spying on his correspondence. The London newspapers had turned hostile to Rousseau, and Hume had done nothing to defend him. Rousseau persisted in suspecting that Hume was the author or an accomplice of the hoax letter from the King of Prussia. Strahan, publisher of *The Saint James's Chronicle,* in which so much hostile matter had been published, was a friend of Hume, and so was young Tronchin, son of Dr Théodore Tronchin of Geneva, who had become one of Rousseau's most bitter enemies. Young Tronchin even lived in the same house as Hume and must be a spy, planted by the government of Geneva to report on him. Hume was a friend of d'Alembert and of the *philosophes* in Paris. So Rousseau's imagination built up a mountain of suspicions that he believed to be facts, which now convinced him that Hume was a traitor to him, in league with his enemies to vilify him in the eyes of the public.

When Rousseau first came to England, Hume knew that his pride would not allow him to live anywhere rent-free. To form some idea of the sum that he might reasonably be expected to pay, Hume thought it his duty in Rousseau's interests to discover what his financial position was. After discreet inquiries from his friends in France, Hume found that the extreme poverty in which Rousseau pretended to live did not truly reflect his actual position, because of the royalties that he received from his very successful books. His poverty must be an affectation. From what he had learnt, Hume suggested the modest sum of £30 a year for Rousseau's and Thérèse's board and lodging. But in view of the sudden, apparent refusal by Rousseau to accept the King's pension, Hume was driven to the conclusion that Rousseau had agreed to steps being taken to obtain it only to be able to renounce it with the greatest ostentation. This confirmed him in his view that Rousseau was nothing but a monster of ingratitude, a vulgar liar and a madman devoured by his own pride and conceit.

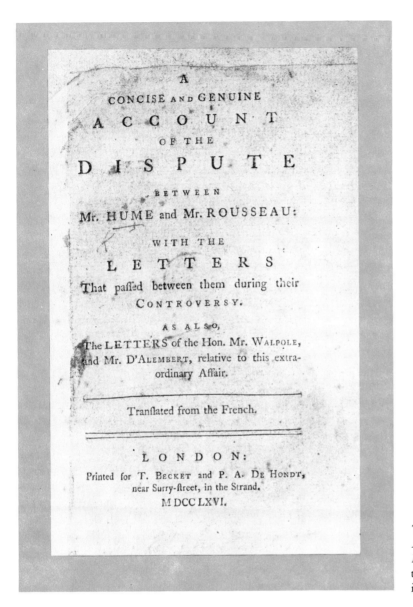

Title-page of the English edition
*Account of the Dispute between Mr.
Hume and Mr. Rousseau* which, with
the French edition, was published
in October 1766

Matters were precipitated when it became known that Rousseau was writing about his 'persecution and defence'. He wrote the first five books of his *Confessions* at Wootton Hall. Then, in a letter of 2 August 1766 to his publisher M. Guy, which somehow found its way into the London newspapers, Rousseau defied Hume to publish any account of the affair without 'enormous falsifications'. After this, Hume felt that he must write *A Concise and genuine Account of the Dispute between Mr Hume and Mr Rousseau*. It consisted mostly of Rousseau's vitriolic letter of 10 July and Hume's comments. Hume considered not letting it be published until after his death. Another letter from Rousseau, of 30 August 1766, which also found its way into the newspapers, denied that he had insultingly refused the King's pension. So Hume's own standing with the King was involved, since the King's name had been brought into the matter publicly. Hume's friends in Paris and in Scotland had advised against immediate publication, Turgot, in particular, pointing out that, however just Hume's indignation might be over Rousseau's behaviour, Hume had misunderstood Rousseau's letter over the King's pension. If Hume published, it could only confirm Rousseau in his suspicions. This was the real tragedy. Each of the two men did exactly what was needed to confirm the suspicions of the other. But Hume had already decided to publish.

Hume's *Concise Account* was sent to Paris, where it was translated into French under the title *Exposé succinct de la contestation qui s'est élevée entre M. Hume et M. Rousseau.* George III and Queen Charlotte were very interested in the case and asked Hume to let them see a copy of his manuscript. The copy which he submitted is in the Royal Library at Windsor, the text in a fine hand, but with marginal notes by Hume himself, some of which are not included in the edition that was finally published. As comments on the different passages of Rousseau's letter to him of 10 July, Hume wrote 'First Lye', 'Second Lye', and so on up to 'Twelfth Lye'; and Hume added, 'Yet this letter [of 10 July] was sealed with Mr Rousseau's usual Motto, *vitam impendere vero*. I ask, Did anyone ever yet know a Pretender to superior Virtue that had Common Honesty?' Hume had lost his temper.

The French and English editions were published in October 1766. This was an occasion not to be missed by Voltaire of turning the knife in Rousseau's wound. He published his *Lettre de M. de Voltaire à M. Hume,* containing the following passage: 'On the dunghill where Rousseau lies, grinding his teeth against the human race, it is permissible to throw him a hunk of bread if he needs it, but it is necessary to make his character known, and to warn those who feed him of his habit of biting their hands.'

In this case, Dr Samuel Johnson agreed with Voltaire about Rousseau: 'I think him one of the worst of men; a rascal, who ought to be hunted out of society, as he has been. Three or four nations have expelled him: and it is a shame that he is protected in this country.... Rousseau, Sir, is a very bad man. I would sooner sign a sentence for his transportation, than that of any felon who has gone from the Old Bailey these many years. Yes, I should like to have him work in the plantations.' This outburst was made to Boswell on 15 February 1766, before any of the trouble between Hume and Rousseau had become known.

Wootton Hall in its isolation, set on the side of a valley with a wide view of trees, fields and rocks, a stream with little waterfalls,

away from towns and other abominations of civilization, where he could wander in solitude and collect plants, was a place after Rousseau's heart. Unfortunately, neither he nor Thérèse could understand the language spoken by the six servants who looked after them, and the day after their arrival, Wootton was buried in snow.

Nature, isolation and solitude were all there, and it seemed possible that Rousseau might stay there indefinitely, for Davenport was willing that he should. Rousseau went for long walks with his dog Sultan, made contact with the lead-miners of Stanton and other simple folk, some of whom still remembered him when William Howitt wrote his *Visits to Remarkable Places*, published in 1840. 'What, owd Ross Hall? Ay know him did I, well enough. Ah've seen him monny an' monny a time, every day welly, coming and going ins comical cap an' ploddy gown, a gathering his yarbs.' 'Yes there war a lady – they cawd her Madam Zell, but whether how war his wife or not, ah dunna know. Folks said how warna.' As at Wotton Place in Surrey, legend grew round Rousseau's stay at Wootton Hall, and with invention passed into folklore. It was said that 'he thought nothing of going over Weaver [Hills] when the *feeris* were out dancing a nights.' Some people took him for an exiled king.

Dovedale, Derbyshire, near Wootton Hall, where Rousseau wandered with his dog Sultan, collecting plants and enjoying the wild scenes of nature

(*Right*) Rousseau botanizing. In the last years of his life, collecting plants was his chief solace from the troubles which he had so largely brought on himself, and made him 'L'homme de la Nature'

(*Below*) View near Carleton, Derbyshire, showing nature after Rousseau's heart

One day when Rousseau was out walking, he met a man looking at a plant, who asked him as he came up if he was a botanist. It was Erasmus Darwin, who knew that Rousseau would pass that way, and so got into conversation with him. But Rousseau suspected that the meeting had been contrived and never let Darwin get near him again.

As had been the case in France, the professional egalitarian had no difficulty in admitting, and getting admitted to, persons of quality in his neighbourhood. At Calwich Abbey there was Bernard Granville, and there Rousseau met Lady Andover, Lady Cowper, Sir Brooke Boothby, Count Orloff and the Duchess of Portland. With Her Grace he went on botanizing excursions on The Peak. He stayed with Davenport at Davenport Hall, and was invited by Lord Strafford to stay in Yorkshire, but it was too far. On 23 February 1767 he visited the Duke of Shrewsbury at Alton.

There was a possibility, of which he never heard, that he might be invited into another ducal family. Ever since the publication of *Émile*, Lady Holland had been enthralled by the book. She admitted that it contained many paradoxes and absurdities, but also more beautiful thoughts than she had found in other books. To her sister, Marchioness of Kildare (afterwards Duchess of Leinster), Lady Holland kept writing to ask if she had read Rousseau. The Duchess needed a tutor for her eldest son, and seriously considered inviting Rousseau to act in this capacity, and to offer him a secluded residence. The Duchess's friends were appalled, and Mrs Delany, sister of Bernard Granville, wrote to Lady Andover on 4 September 1766 to draw attention to the fact that while 'The Rousseau was a genius and a curiosity', he was dangerous for young minds, because 'under the *guise and pomp of virtue*' he professed false and heterodox opinions, and that it was best to entrust children to a '*downright honest parson*'. No more was heard of Rousseau's becoming tutor to the Duchess's son.

On 22 January 1767, the Duke of Grafton, Prime Minister, remitted the Customs duty of £15 that had been charged for Rousseau's box of books. He sent the money to the subscription raised in London for the aid of the poor in Geneva, further impoverished by the blockade which the French army had imposed on the city because of the riots between the political parties, the 'représentants' and the 'négatifs', trouble which Rousseau had started with his *Lettres écrites de la montagne*.

At the stage of life that he had reached, Rousseau's greatest need was to justify himself to himself, and to posterity. This was what he intended to do in his *Confessions*, which he had started to write at Môtiers-Travers, and now continued at Wootton Hall. But a new panic assailed him. He convinced himself that his manuscript would never be allowed to leave England, because he was sure that

Erasmus Darwin, physician, poet and polymath, grandfather of Charles Darwin and of Francis Galton. Near Wootton Hall he succeeded in getting into conversation with Rousseau over collecting plants; but Rousseau suspected that the meeting had been contrived and he refused to have anything more to do with Darwin

The market-place at Spalding,
Lincolnshire, showing the White
Hart Inn, the third house on the
right. Rousseau stayed there after he
had left Wootton Hall in May 1767

Hume's invitation was only a trap to keep him in England. His
own freedom, he feared, was not assured. He suspected the house-
keeper and the servants at Wootton Hall of opening his letters and
putting cinders in his food. Next he suspected Davenport, and
wrote him a furious letter demanding to know immediately on what
footing he stood in his house. Davenport returned a soft answer, and
the rift appeared to have been mended. In March 1767, to the great
surprise of General Conway, Rousseau applied through Davenport
for the promised pension from George III. It was granted on
18 March.

The winter of 1766–67 was particularly severe, and Rousseau
sank into a new frenzy of despair and persecution-mania because
Davenport (who had been ill) failed to return from London and
visit him. On 1 May 1767, after writing to Davenport regretting
that he could not make him a true friend, Rousseau and Thérèse
suddenly left Wootton Hall, leaving their luggage behind, and no
address. On 5 May they turned up at Spalding in Lincolnshire,
where they stayed at the White Hart Inn. The unbalanced state of
Rousseau's mind is shown by his behaviour there. His reason for
coming to Lincolnshire was to hand the famous manuscript of the
Confessions to a trustworthy Swiss, Maximilien de Cerjat, who lived
at Louth, and would send it to du Peyrou at Neuchâtel. By this

92

means he avoided the danger that the manuscript would be found on him and confiscated. On the same day, 5 May, Rousseau addressed a letter to the Lord Chancellor, Lord Camden, asking for protection against the dangers by which he felt surrounded and menaced, and he asked for a guard to accompany him to Dover.

From Spalding, Rousseau also wrote to Davenport on 11 May, saying, 'I preferred liberty to a residence in your house. But I infinitely prefer a residence in your house to any other form of captivity, and I prefer every kind of captivity to that in which I am, which is horrible and unendurable, come what may.'

In spite of the panic and despair in which Rousseau professed to be, the local clergyman, the Rev. John Dinham, found him every day 'cheerful, good-humoured, easy, and enjoying himself perfectly well, without the least fear or complaint of any kind.'

Assuming that he was not an actor, it might be asked if Rousseau was schizophrenic, but he was probably not. His powers of imagination were so great, his timidity so marked, his moral indignation so easy to inflame, his vanity so overwhelming, and his egotism so unassailable, that at one moment he might be violently defensive and hostile and at the next a peaceful, apparently normal man, almost in a state of euphoria. There is an additional, more serious explanation of his behaviour. He was showing incipient signs of insanity. John Locke pointed out that the difference between a muddle-headed fool and a madman is that the fool cannot reason logically even from correct premises, while the madman reasons with unerring logic from premises that are wholly wrong or non-existent. With Rousseau, it was the imagined international conspiracy, led by Voltaire, Hume and all the others, that unhinged him. The tragedy was that he needed this conspiracy to justify himself to himself, for at the back of his mind there were always those unpardonable things that he had done, stealing the ribbon and blaming Marion, and abandoning his children. As he had also convinced himself that he was 'good', the best of men, he carried about with him an internal conflict; this he tried to resolve by pleading that he had atoned for those early misdeeds by the suffering to which he had been subjected, by his bodily ailments and the persecution at the hands of the 'conspiracy'. Horace Walpole summed him up unerringly in his hoax letter from the King of Prussia: Rousseau feared and at the same time courted persecution. He had been outlawed in France, Geneva and Berne; he had been stoned out of Môtiers-Travers, but in England he had no valid cause for any apprehension at all, apart from figments of his own disordered and exaggerated imagination.

When Davenport received Rousseau's letter from Spalding, he immediately sent a servant to assure Rousseau of his continued protection and freedom to live at Wootton Hall. But Rousseau had

Charles Pratt, Lord Camden, Lord High Chancellor. Suffering from persecution mania, Rousseau wrote to him asking for protection from the dangers by which he thought himself surrounded, and for a guard to escort him to Dover

The portrait of Rousseau painted by Allan Ramsay for David Hume in 1766. Rousseau included this portrait, 'making him look like a Cyclops', among his griefs against David Hume

left Spalding on 14 May, and arrived at Dover on 16 May. He wrote to General Conway, imploring to be allowed to leave England unmolested, in spite of the 'conspiracy' by which he had been inveigled to England to dishonour him. Rousseau also wrote to Davenport to say that when he saw the sea, he realized that he was a free man after all, and resolved to return to Wootton Hall. But the newspapers were so critical of the manner in which he had deserted Wootton Hall that he gave up the idea. His mind became clouded again. The wind at Dover was adverse, and he felt that Heaven was now in league with his enemies. In a dish that was served to him containing parsley, he mistook the parsley for hemlock. On 21 May at dinner time, he rushed out of the inn terrified, went on board the ship which was still high and dry at low tide, and locked himself in a cabin. By now he suspected even Thérèse, and she had the greatest difficulty in getting him to come on shore again. They embarked and set sail that night.

The copy of the portrait of Rousseau painted for Richard Davenport by Allan Ramsay in 1767 for £20. A comparison with the original portrait of 1766 shows a difference of expression, and is probably more lifelike

In spite of his professed ingratitude, his former friends in England had greater regard for Rousseau than he gave them credit for. Hume had supported Davenport's petition for the King's pension to be granted to him. When it became clear that Rousseau was making for France, with all the dangers for him that this involved, Hume wrote to Turgot and asked him to use his best endeavours with Malesherbes to give Rousseau protection in France. Turgot replied that it was because the request came from Hume that the Duc de Choiseul, Prime Minister, stood the best chance of obtaining this favour from Louis xv.

Davenport ordered a copy from Allan Ramsay of the portrait that he had painted of Rousseau for Hume, and paid £20 for it. In fact, Ramsay sent him two copies, different in expression from the original canvas and probably more lifelike. Another copy was taken to Catton Hall by Davenport's grand-daughter Phoebe, who married Christopher Norton. A fourth copy, attributed to Thomas

Nuneham Courtenay, Oxfordshire, where Lord Nuneham established a little 'Rousseau Museum' in honour of his friend whom he admired so much, containing a portrait and a bust of Rousseau

Gauguin, was placed by Lord Nuneham in the little 'Rousseau Museum' that he had set up at Nuneham Courtenay, where there was also a bust of Rousseau with an inscription by Sir Brooke Boothby. Yet another, very bad copy of Ramsay's portrait is in the Château de Coppet; Mme de Staël must have found it in London during her stay and taken it home with her.

There must be other relics of Rousseau in England. He made his will at Wootton Hall and gave it to Davenport on 26 May 1766. Davenport's executor, Edward Mainwaring, showed it to Lord Bagot, but it has not been traced. Nor have the books of Rousseau's library, which he sold on 12 March 1767 to Louis Dutens, a Frenchman in the British diplomatic service, who gave him an annuity of £10 for them.

When Rousseau and Thérèse landed at Calais on 22 May 1767, he did not know where to go. He thought of Brussels, and then of Venice; but he had no passport for travelling through France and the warrant for his arrest was still in force. He wrote to the Prince de Conti to ask his advice and said that he would wait for his reply at Amiens. The Prince told him that he was in grave danger, not so much from the court, the King, or the Duc de Choiseul, as from the Parlement of Paris. A single zealous underling, eager for promotion, could denounce him, and the law would then have to take its course. He was advised to leave Amiens quietly and at night. At the inn at Saint-Denis he called himself M. Jacques. The Marquis de Mirabeau had him and Thérèse escorted from there to

(*Above*) Amiens, the Chaussée Saint-Leu with the Hôtel Dieu on the right and the cathedral in the background. Rousseau was advised by the Prince de Conti to leave Amiens secretly by night

(*Left*) Abbeville, showing the cathedral. After leaving Calais, Rousseau went about openly in Abbeville, which was imprudent as, only a few years before, the Chevalier de la Barre had been the victim of one of the most atrocious judicial tortures and murders in France, on religious grounds

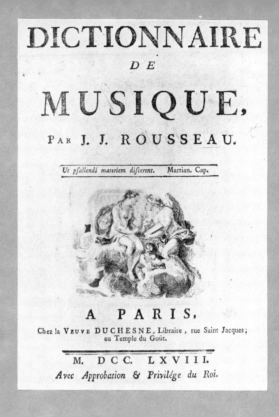

(*Left*) Louis-François de Bourbon, Prince de Conti, Rousseau's most powerful and steadfast protector in France. He was the first French prince of the blood royal to refuse the rites of the Catholic Church at his death, in 1776

Title-page of Rousseau's *Dictionnaire de Musique*, 1768, on which he worked for many years

his own house at Fleury-sous-Meudon, where they stayed a fortnight. Rousseau's old friend from Geneva, François Coindet, then escorted them to the Prince de Conti's château of Trye-le-Château near Gisors.

It was almost like Wootton Hall all over again. There was trouble with the servants, who despised a guest without gold lace, a plume or a sword. There were soul-storms over imaginary dangers and breaks with friends. Coindet called again, but as he worked for the Paris banker Necker (father of Mme de Staël), he inclined towards the 'négatifs' in Geneva politics and against the 'représentants', so Rousseau fell out with him.

The Prince de Conti insisted that Rousseau must protect himself by adopting the name of Jean-Joseph Renou: Thérèse was to become his sister, Mlle Renou. Rousseau then had a fearful battle with himself on whether to leave or to stay. It was an urge to escape, but as it was himself that he really needed to escape from, the problem was insoluble. He decided to remain where he was. Presently his great friend Pierre-Alexandre du Peyrou, from Neuchâtel, came to stay, bringing with him the precious manuscript of the *Confessions* which he had received safely from Maximilien de Cerjat in Lincolnshire. He also brought a copy of Rousseau's *Dictionnaire de musique*.

98

An attack of gout made du Peyrou very ill, and Rousseau got it into his head that du Peyrou suspected Rousseau of having poisoned him. Rousseau's disordered imagination then led him to fall out with du Peyrou over the affairs of Geneva, which Rousseau could not leave alone. Du Peyrou recovered and left, but not before Rousseau had annulled the contract by which du Peyrou paid him a pension. Further trouble arose when a new porter employed at the château died. He had always been on bad terms with Rousseau, and locked him in or locked him out to be tiresome. During the porter's illness, Thérèse had made him some soup, and Rousseau now feared that he would be suspected of having poisoned the porter. All this toxiphobia, at Wootton Hall, at Dover and at Trye-le-Château, is a sign of mental derangement.

On 10 June 1768, Rousseau left Trye-le-Château, alone, as suddenly as he had left Wootton Hall. He made his way to Lyons, where he still had some friends, and went on a botanical excursion

Lyons from the Quai Saint-Antoine. This town played a large part in Rousseau's life; it was where he learnt to copy music for a living in 1731, served as tutor to the sons of M. de Mably in 1740, and stayed in 1768 after leaving Trye-le-Château. In 1770 his opera *Pygmalion* was performed there at the town hall

(*Opposite*) The monastery of the Grande Chartreuse, in its setting of mountains where Rousseau went on botanizing excursions in 1768

Thérèse Levasseur in old age. During the French Revolution, her association with Rousseau made her a person of honour and distinction

to the mountains around the Grande Chartreuse. On 25 July he made a pilgrimage to the cemetery at Lemenc, near Chambéry, where Mme de Warens was buried. Her grave was neglected and overgrown with weeds. After a stay at Grenoble he went in August to the little town of Bourgoin and took rooms at the Fontaine d'Or, where Thérèse joined him on 26 August.

Four days later, there took place the most absurd and pathetic ceremony imaginable. Rousseau had invited the mayor of Bourgoin and one of his friends to the inn, without telling them why, or what was going to happen. When they arrived, they found Rousseau and Thérèse dressed for a wedding. It was to be their own (by which Rousseau went back on his original promise to Thérèse). But what made it such a farcical parody of the most important ceremony in life was that Rousseau officiated himself. The ritual 'I do' was pronounced by the bridegroom and bride, and Rousseau made an impassioned speech, after which everybody burst into tears.

Thérèse's luggage had not arrived from Trye-le-Château, and Rousseau saw in this yet another villainy by his enemies, to reduce him to beggary and want. The luggage came, but another storm broke. It was the 'affaire Thévenin'. Nicolas-Émile Thévenin was a gaol-bird and swindler who alleged that Rousseau owed him nine francs, borrowed ten years previously at an inn near Neu-châtel. By means of affidavits, which took weeks to arrive, Rous-seau was able to prove that he was at Montmorency when the alleged loan was said to have been made, and that Thévenin had previously been condemned to the galleys. But it had meant employing a lawyer, appealing to the governor of the province, and going through an agony of worry.

In a delirium of self-pity and persecution-mania, Rousseau then convinced himself that the Thévenin affair was not accidental, but had been organized by the 'conspiracy' of his enemies to test him, to see if he still reacted. On a number of grounds, he now pin-pointed the leader of his foes as the Duc de Choiseul. There was the disparaging passage against ministers of monarchies in his *Contrat social*, with the sentence intended to except Choiseul from his strictures, but which Choiseul had clearly not recognized. There were, next, two steps of foreign policy which Choiseul took in that year, 1768, which Rousseau had reached a sufficient stage of vanity to think were aimed directly against him. One was the dispatch of a French army to Corsica, which was a perfectly normal operation since France had made a treaty with Genoa for the sovereignty over Corsica. But Rousseau could not forget that he, Rousseau, only four years previously, had been invited to draft a constitution for Corsica. The second grievance was that Choiseul had planned to make the village of Versoix, then French, on the Lake of Geneva, a town and trade-centre to rival and ruin Geneva.

Étienne-François, Duc de Choiseul, Prime Minister of France, whom Rousseau, demented with persecution mania, thought was the leader of his personal enemies

A prey again to his chimeras, Rousseau thought of escaping to Cyprus, or to Minorca, both of them islands, for which he had such predilection, or to America. He even thought of going back to Wootton Hall. Then the pendulum swung again, and he decided to remain in France. But he reflected that the only times when he had been happy were when he was really poor. Accordingly, he renounced his pension from George III. For Rousseau, money was certainly the source of nearly all evil, because, as he said in *Émile*, 'it is the true link of society'; it corrupts both him who gives and him who receives, and turns the latter into a slave because it puts him under the obligation of gratitude.

Rousseau and Thérèse fell ill, and attributed this to the damp climate of Bourgoin. A local lady bountifully offered them one of her farms at Monquin, a village a few miles from Bourgoin, on the heights in full view of the Alps, and they moved in at the end of January 1769. In August, there seems to have been a rift between Rousseau and Thérèse, probably attributable to the fact that, just as at Môtiers-Travers and at Wootton Hall, Thérèse was bored stiff at Monquin, so far away from Paris and everything that she knew. Rousseau then went on another botanical excursion, this time to the Mont Pilat in the province of Vivarais, on the other side of the Rhône. But it was too late for flowers, one of his companions was bitten by a dog, his own dog Sultan was involved in a fight and disappeared, and it rained without stopping. On his return to Monquin, Rousseau found Thérèse somewhat reconciled, and also Sultan who had managed somehow to cross the Rhône and find his way home.

What Rousseau sighed for was a spinet, for he said, 'Music for me is a true remedy, and perhaps the only one in my present state.'

Entrance to the farm at Monquin, near Bourgoin, Isère, where Rousseau lived in 1769

The Café Procope, 13 rue de l'Ancienne Comédie, Paris, a favourite resort of writers and frequented by Rousseau

Mme Boy de la Tour sent him one from Lyons. In sec.et he continued to work at his *Confessions,* of which he had written the sixth book at Trye-le-Château. He now started on the last six books of the second part, which covered his life in Paris and his expulsion from France. This return to his own defence in face of posterity had a curious effect. It gave him courage. The Prince de Conti had repeated his warning that Rousseau must continue to call himself Renou and to take all precautions against denunciation. One of his mental tortures had been that, try as he might, he was unable to get to grips with his imaginary persecutors. The more he tried, the more he found himself enveloped in a fog of impenetrable anonymity and silence. He now decided to step out and challenge the world under his own name of Jean-Jacques Rousseau.

The first step in this counter-offensive was to leave Monquin for Lyons. He met a musician there, and together they set to music his poem *Pygmalion,* which was performed in the town hall on 19 April 1770. On the way to Paris Rousseau called on the naturalist Buffon at Montbard and had a very good reception. On 24 June he arrived in Paris and put up at the Hôtel du Saint-Esprit in his old rue Plâtrière. He now wore French clothes and frequented the Café de la Régence (161 rue Saint-Honoré) and the Café Procope (13 rue de l'Ancienne-Comédie), where all writers and *litterati* went. His return caused some sensation. He resumed his work of copying music to earn his living. In December he received a visit from Charles Burney the musician, whose daughter Fanny told George III that the first thing her father saw in Rousseau's room was a portrait of his royal benefactor. Voltaire was furious. Under a political cloud himself, he asked how it was possible for a man against whom an arrest warrant was outstanding, should be in Paris and he, Voltaire, not.

(*Right*) The Salon of Madame Geoffrin. She is on the right (11), sitting on the Prince de Conti's (10) left; in the centre, reading, is the actor Le Kain (5), on the right of whom is d'Alembert (7); at the back on a pedestal is a bust of Voltaire (6), to the right of which are Diderot (8) and Turgot (9); in front of the door Rousseau (3) is talking to Rameau (4); on the left is Buffon (2), with Condillac (1) behind him; on the extreme right is the Comtesse d'Houdetot (12)

(*Below*) The first page of the manuscript of Rousseau's *Confessions*. Begun at Wootton Hall, continued at Trye-le-Château and Monquin, it was not published until after his death

I. :des Confessions de J. J. Rousseau.
Prémière Partie.
Livre I.

Intùs, et in Cute.

1. Je forme une entreprise qui n'eut jamais d'exemple, et dont l'exécution n'aura point d'imitateur. Je veux montrer à mes semblables un homme dans toute la vérité de la nature; et cet homme, ce sera moi.

2. Moi seul. Je sens mon cœur et je connois les hommes. Je ne suis fait comme aucun de ceux que j'ai vus; j'ose croire n'être fait comme aucun de ceux qui existent. Si je ne vaux pas mieux, au moins je suis autre. Si la nature a bien ou mal fait de briser le moule dans lequel elle m'a jetté, c'est ce dont on ne peut juger qu'après m'avoir lû.

3. Que la trompette du jugement dernier sonne quand elle voudra; je viendrai ce livre à la main me présenter devant le souverain juge. Je dirai hautement: voilà ce que j'ai fait, ce que j'ai pensé ce que je fus. J'ai dit le bien et le mal avec la même franchise. Je n'ai rien tu de mauvais, rien ajouté de bon, et s'il m'est arrivé d'employer quelque ornement indifférent, ce n'a jamais été que pour remplir un vide occasionné par mon défaut de mémoire; j'ai pu supposer vrai ce que je savois avoir pû l'être, jamais ce que je savois être faux. Je me suis montré tel que je fus, méprisable et vil quand je l'ai été, bon, généreux sublime, quand je l'ai été: j'ai dévoilé mon intérieur tel

Towards the end of 1770, the manuscript of the *Confessions* was finished. Its narrative stopped at Rousseau's expulsion from the Île Saint-Pierre, and contained nothing more recent. In that remarkable book Rousseau confessed to the misdeeds that lay so heavily on his conscience, but on comparing the text with contemporary documents, many of them his own letters, it can be seen that he managed to twist his descriptions of events so that he emerged as the innocent party, shamefully treated by others. In some places he lied, in others his memory was faulty, but always in his favour. It was a whitewashing operation, with a few confessions thrown in, to show how honest he was.

There is a marked difference in style between the *Confessions* and the other books he published. The latter were polemical and aggressive, written for his contemporaries. The *Confessions* were written for posterity, to ingratiate himself in the eyes of unborn generations who would, he was convinced, 'love him'.

It seems that the Public Prosecutor in Paris warned him that he must not publish anything. But nothing had been said about his reading passages from his *Confessions* in the salons of fashionable hostesses. Many a tear was shed when he read about his theft of the ribbon, and about the abandonment of his children. One reading, which the poet Claude-Joseph Dorat attended, lasted from nine o'clock in the morning until three in the morning of the next day.

Antoine de Sartine,
Lieutenant-Général de Police, the
most feared man in Paris, who
nevertheless treated Rousseau most
humanely

This reading of the *Confessions* alarmed Mme d'Épinay, and she asked the Lieutenant de Police, M. de Sartine, to speak to Rousseau gently and get him to promise that he would not read in public any more. That he was not summarily thrown into the Bastille is proof of the considerate manner in which the authorities treated him.

Balked of having his *Confessions* printed, or even of reading them, he was deprived of the means of justifying himself, and became even more boorish to his friends. He had now quarrelled with nearly all the old ones and refused, with one or two exceptions, to make new ones. He refused to receive and pay postage on letters addressed to him unless he recognized the handwriting. Driven in more and more on himself, 'on earth only to weep', his only comfort lay in occasional botanical excursions, in the outskirts of Paris. He complained that botany books were of use only to those who already knew botany, and he started writing his *Lettres sur la botanique*, addressed to Mme Delessert, daughter of Mme Boy de la Tour. They were beautifully written, but no new contribution to science. He still made little herbaria, for some of which he exchanged plants with the Duchess of Portland.

Towards the end of 1771, Rousseau moved into a small flat on the fifth floor of an apartment building in the rue Plâtrière, where fashionable ladies, disguised as servants, came to bring him music to copy, if they could get past Thérèse who mounted a strict guard at the door.

At about this time, Rousseau received a visit from a Polish count, Michel Wielhorsky, asking him to suggest ways of reforming the government of Poland which was in a very bad way, and about to suffer its first partition between Prussia, Russia and Austria. So Rousseau returned to his hobby of constitution-making and drew up an essay which became *Considérations sur le Gouvernement de Pologne*, but was of course not published until after his death. In this curious work, Rousseau made himself the apostle of nationalism. 'Today', he said, 'there are no more Frenchmen, Germans, Spaniards, or even Englishmen, but only Europeans. All have the same tastes, passions, habits...under similar circumstances, each will do the same thing.... A child on opening his eyes, should see his own nation, and until his death, nothing but his own nation.' So, Rousseau concluded, the only remedy for the troubles of Poland was to instil a sentiment of Polish nationalism, so that Poles should be different from other nationals. In this pitiable work – where his inexorable logic, applied to false premises, came to such deplorable conclusions – he expressed the hope that all nations would adopt the same policy.

More and more depressed and repressed, always hankering after his justification, he found solace in writing one of the most extraordinary works in the world. Universally known by his Christian

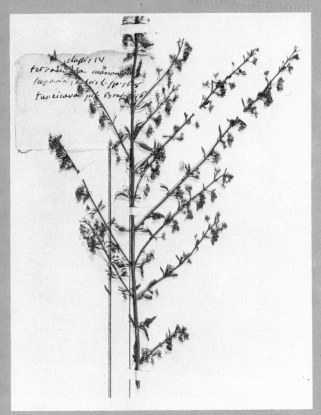

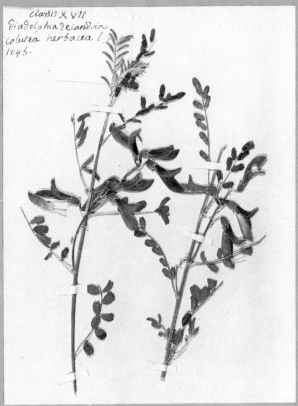

names of Jean-Jacques, he resented the fact that the public had
deprived him of his surname of Rousseau, but this suggested to him
a novel form of dialectic. Rousseau, under his own surname, argues
with an imaginary Frenchman about himself, referred to as Jean-
Jacques. This gives Rousseau a final opportunity of attacking the
'conspiracy' against him, of justifying himself and giving himself
absolution. The Frenchman advances all the arguments that could
be levelled against Jean-Jacques, and Rousseau parries them.
Finally, the Frenchman agrees with Rousseau that Jean-Jacques's
life and works have been inspired by the same virtue. This was the
gist of *Dialogues, Rousseau juge de Jean-Jacques.*

This extraordinary document also enabled Rousseau to bring to
the front an idea which had long been in his mind, and had become
a conviction. He hints at nothing less than that his life was a sort of
parallel with that of Jesus. At the beginning of the *Confessions*, he
defied all men on the Day of Judgment, standing before the throne
of the Almighty, to claim that they were better than he was. Further
on in the same book, he boasted quite openly, 'I who have always

Rousseau in the Cathedral of Notre-Dame de Paris, trying in vain to lay the manuscript of his *Dialogues, Rousseau juge de Jean-Jacques* on the high altar, 24 February 1776

The Abbé de Condillac, to whom Rousseau gave his manuscript to read but received no encouragement

thought and still think myself the best of men.' In a letter to Malesherbes, he claimed that 'of all the men I have known in my life, I am firmly persuaded that none was better than I'.

The parallel went further. Jesus failed to convert the Jewish people; Rousseau failed to convert French and Swiss society. Jesus suffered; Rousseau suffered. Jesus was persecuted; Rousseau imagined himself as persecuted. Orthodox theology believes in the Fall of Man and in the possibility of Redemption by the Saviour. Rousseau proclaimed his own form of the Fall of Man, due to the effects of society which depraved Man from his original non-social condition. Mankind was in need of a saviour to lead it back to innocence and nature. This saviour was Rousseau himself. It was impossible for any man to hold such views without sinking into melancholic monomania.

Having written his *Dialogues*, the question arose what to do with it, as he could not publish it. Carried away by his proof of his own innocence and of the iniquity of the 'conspirators', he decided to entrust his manuscript to God himself, by placing it on the high altar of Notre-Dame de Paris. The sensation that this action would cause might even bring his document to the notice of the King. This idea is further evidence of his mental derangement. He was in the bad books of the Catholic hierarchy, and his plan of action was the surest method of getting his manuscript consigned to the flames. On 24 February 1776 he went to the cathedral with his document, but found that access to the high altar was barred by locked gates.

Rousseau regarded this rebuff as further proof that the Powers of the Spirit were allied to his enemies. He must find another way of drawing attention to his tragedy. On the following day he gave his precious manuscript to his old friend Condillac, the philosopher, to read; but Condillac was cold about it, and criticized it as if it were a work of philosophy. Rousseau took it back. Then it happened that Sir Brooke Boothby, his neighbour at Wootton Hall, called on him, and in a fit of confidence, Rousseau entrusted the manuscript of the first *Dialogue* to Boothby. Quickly afterwards, Rousseau regretted that he had left this evidence of his own martyrdom in the hands of an Englishman, a man whose country had treated him so

Sir Brooke Boothby, Bart, who had been a neighbour of Rousseau when he was at Wootton Hall. Passing through Paris in 1776 he called on Rousseau who gave him the manuscript of the first *Dialogue*, to be published after his death, which Boothby did, at Lichfield, in 1781

(*Left*) One of the handbills written and distributed to passers-by in the streets, in Paris, by Rousseau, entitled 'To every Frenchman who still loves justice and truth'

(*Above*) Notes for Rousseau's *Rêveries du Promeneur Solitaire*, his last and unfinished work, written on the back of a playing card

badly and must be in league with his enemies. He need not have worried, for Brooke Boothby was conscientiousness itself, and faithfully published the *Dialogue* (at Lichfield) after Rousseau's death.

The sequel was the most poignant evidence of the misery which Rousseau now suffered. He wrote with his own hand a large number of handbills, headed 'To every Frenchman who still loves justice and truth'. He stood at street corners and tried to thrust a copy into the hands of passers-by who struck him as honest. They refused to accept it, saying after they had read the heading that it was not for them. Had they read its contents they would have found enough to have him arrested: 'Frenchmen, members of a nation once lovable and sweet, what have you become? How changed you are for an unfortunate foreigner, alone, at your mercy and without help or defender, but who would not need either among a just people.... Abandon that old name of *Francs*: it must make you blush too much.' This was his last attempt to discover what he was accused of, and why he was persecuted. It was in tune with another remark that he made: 'The Swiss will never forgive me for the harm that they have done to me.'

During a popular demonstration in the street which had nothing to do with him, a straw man was burned. Rousseau of course inferred that it was meant for him. On 24 October 1776, on returning from a walk near Ménilmontant, he was knocked down in the street by a great dog that accompanied a nobleman's carriage rushing down the slope. He fainted, and when he recovered he interpreted the event as meaning that he had not yet suffered enough. Rumours spread that he had been killed, and some papers even published obituary notices of him, from which Rousseau was able to see what his enemies would make of the event when it really happened.

After this accident and the shock he suffered, Rousseau became calm and quiet, 'poor unfortunate mortal', he wrote, 'as impassive as God himself'. He took to his pen once more, and wrote the *Rêveries du Promeneur Solitaire*. In many ways these *Rêveries* (of which there were ten, the last unfinished) were the most beautiful prose that he wrote. The fifth, which was devoted to his blessed times on the Île Saint-Pierre, contained the first use in French of the word *romantique* as applied to scenery, in this particular case the shores of the Lake of Bienne. This is a reminder of the part which Rousseau's works were to play in stimulating the Romantic movement.

Louis-Réné, Marquis de Girardin, Rousseau's last benefactor who gave him a house on his estate at Ermenonville

The first *Rêverie* was less felicitous. It began, 'Here, then, am I, left alone on earth, without brother, kin, friend, or any society but myself.' No thought for Thérèse, who during a third of a century had trailed after him as faithfully as a dog and nursed him, and he cannot have been an easy man to live with. His principle of never showing gratitude applied even to her, his wife in his own eyes. He had become so fond of himself that nobody else mattered. By the same token, there was nothing but ingratitude for the many who had exerted themselves for his benefit and protection: the Luxembourgs, Prince de Conti, Malesherbes, and his old friend Paul Moultou of Geneva, who came to Paris on 2 May 1788 to take charge of Rousseau's manuscripts, to publish them in a consolidated edition, in collaboration with du Peyrou.

Rousseau had reached the age when he could not copy music any longer, and was worried to know how he could earn his daily bread. The Marquis de Girardin offered him a retreat in his magnificent domain of Ermenonville, where a cottage was to be built for him. While waiting for it to be ready, he was to live in a small pavilion near the big house. On 26 May, Rousseau and Thérèse settled in. Four days later, Voltaire died a painful death in Paris, and Rousseau was all the more shaken because Jean-Hyacinth Magalhaens was at Ermenonville; he had been an eyewitness of the Lisbon earthquake in 1755 and described it. This reminded Rousseau forcibly of his old quarrel with his enemy Voltaire.

(*Above*) The Park and Château of
Ermenonville where, while a guest of
the Marquis de Girardin, Rousseau
died 2 July 1778

(*Right*) Rousseau's tomb on the Île
des Peupliers in the lake of the park
at Ermenonville

On 2 July 1778, four days after his sixty-sixth birthday, Rousseau went for a walk in the morning, and was getting ready to give a music lesson to Girardin's daughter, when he complained of pins-and-needles in his feet, a cold chill down his spine, discomfort in his chest and violent pains in the head. At eleven o'clock he died, of apoplexy. He was buried on 4 July in a tomb on the Île des Peupliers, a tiny island in the lake in the Park of Ermenonville. At last he was in solitude, isolated on a small island.

Rousseau was dead, and his world, in so far as France and Switzer-land were concerned, was to endure a few more years, until it was plunged into the melting-pot of the French Revolution, to which his ideas had contributed in many ways. Nobody would have been more horrified than he at the misapplication of his ideas, dangerous things, in the excesses perpetrated in that great upheaval.

Rousseau's death mask

Although his accent can be heard clearly in the Declaration of the Rights of Man, Rousseau was not in the earliest ranks of the acknowledged prophets of the French Revolution. In political esteem, his enemy Voltaire came before him, because Voltaire's anti-clericalism, his campaign against the Roman Catholic Church, his crusade for tolerance, and general undermining of the establish-ment, by the massive number and weight of his works, prepared progressive opinion for the clean sweep which would put an end to the *ancien régime*. The Constituent Assembly ordered that Voltaire's remains should be transferred from the Abbaye de Scellières to the Panthéon in Paris, the edifice destined to become the mausoleum of great French revolutionaries. The event took place on 12 July 1791. In the same year, the Quai des Théatins, on which was the house where Voltaire died (1 rue de Beaune), became the Quai Voltaire, and the rue Plâtrière in which Rousseau had lived became the rue Jean-Jacques Rousseau.

Rousseau's turn to be 'panthéonisé' came later, when power had been seized by the Jacobins. The Girondins had wanted a federal, regionalized France, but Rousseau, in his *Contrat social*, had pro-claimed that sovereignty is 'indivisible', and this became the slogan of the Jacobins, *République française, une et indivisible*. Jean-Paul Marat, another Swiss, was then reading passages from the *Contrat social* in the street, and the Reign of Terror was sending thousands to the drownings, shootings and the guillotine. Among the victims was Antoine-Laurent Lavoisier, founder of modern chemistry, who was executed on 8 May 1794. To a plea for stay of execution in order that he might finish some important experiments, the judge, Coffinhal, replied: 'The Republic has no need of scientists.' One wonders whether this reply was in any way prompted by Rousseau's denunciation of science as responsible for the depravity of man, in his first *Discours*.

(*Right*) The church of Sainte Geneviève, Paris, converted by the authorities into the Panthéon, destined to receive the mortal remains of heroes of the French Revolution, including Voltaire and Rousseau, and (*below*) the temporary mausoleum erected in the Tuileries Gardens to receive Rousseau's remains on 10 October 1794, on their way from Ermenonville to the Panthéon

The Convention ordered that Rousseau's remains be transferred to the Panthéon, and on 9 October 1794 they were removed from the Île des Peupliers at Ermenonville, on the way to Paris. On the following day they were temporarily housed in a mausoleum specially erected for them in the Tuileries Gardens, and on the 11th they were carried in procession to the Panthéon. They were preceded by Captain Joshua Barney, U.S.N., carrying a banner of the Stars and Stripes, leading a column of Americans. The United States Minister James Monroe, and his suite, were the only persons admitted to the Panthéon with the members of the Convention. Voltaire and Rousseau would have been horrified at the thought of their close association in the same building; but it did not last for long, because after the restoration of the Bourbons in 1814, their remains were removed and scattered.

Considering the parallel lines of ideas on freedom and equality that moved in the minds of Rousseau and of the Founding Fathers of the United States, it might have been expected that some influence of Rousseau's thought should be traceable in the Declaration of Independence of 4 July 1776, or at least in the work of the Constitutional Congress of 17 September 1787. Paul Merrill Spurlin's study shows that none is to be found; 'Rousseau had vogue but no influence in eighteenth-century America.' John Adams heaped ridicule on Rousseau's *Discours*; John Quincy Adams said of the *Contrat social* that it was 'neither practicable nor metaphysically true'.

It may be that a more subtle indirect influence by Rousseau on America can be found in the mental evolution of Benjamin Franklin. He was in England at the same time as Rousseau in 1766.

(*Left*) Benjamin Franklin, whose ideas were probably influenced by Rousseau's rejection of technology and manufacturing industry, and the enthusiasm of the *Physiocrates* for agriculture, the combined result of which was to sever the connection between industrial England and the agricultural States of New England

(*Right*) Jean-Paul Marat, the 'Ami du Peuple', who gave readings in the streets of Rousseau's *Contrat social* during the French Revolution. Born at Boudry, near Neuchâtel, he was murdered by Charlotte Corday in Paris

In those days Franklin was a loyal British subject, endeavouring to obtain economic autonomy for the American colonies, and no imposition of 'internal taxes' from across the Atlantic. But after a visit to France, when he met Rousseau's friend the Marquis de Mirabeau, and François Quesnay, the leader of the *physiocrates*, Franklin reflected that there were three ways by which a state could enrich itself: first, by war, capture and brigandage; second, by commerce, most often swindle; third, by agriculture, the only honest means by which a man can increase his wealth through the forces of nature. This was the creed of the *physiocrates*. England, industrializing herself, was becoming 'rotten' and on the way to corruption, down the slope of depravity described by Rousseau in his first *Discours* on the fatal results of arts and sciences. In his third *Dialogue* (which Franklin could not have read as it was not published) Rousseau wrote, 'it is easy to foresee that in twenty years from now, England with all her glory will be ruined, and will have lost the rest of her freedom.' America, on the other hand, depending on agriculture, as Franklin saw, was sane and virtuous. This antithesis between manufacture and technology in towns, and agriculture in the country, was exactly what Rousseau had preached since his first *Discours*, and may have converted Franklin into a rebel, to free the American colonies from dependence on British manufactured goods, and to preserve American morals and liberty.

It is not possible in such small space to do justice to the effect of Rousseau's ideas on morals, sociology, politics, religion and literature. One of the difficulties is that he was a bundle of inconsistencies and contradictions. Literature and printing, he asserted, were curses to mankind, yet he became a prolific author. When man 'distanced himself from the animal state' and began to have ideas, he set the seal on his unhappiness, yet few men have had more ideas than he. Living with a mistress and having had a previous score of three women, he sang the praises of chaste conjugal love. Devoted to women, he wrote of them as an anti-feminist. Placing his children in a foundling hospital instead of bringing them up, he provided a blueprint of educational policy. Author of many plays, he thundered against theatres. Attacking the great, the titled and the rich, he remained dependent on them for protection, shelter and subsistence.

Rousseau was not unaware of his internal inconsistencies, and he justified them as he justified everything else about himself. In this case he appealed to what he called his *morale sensitive*, by which he meant the different effects produced on the mind by changed sensations and situations. To d'Alembert on the subject of theatres he replied that you could say things in Paris that you could not say in Geneva. This was in accordance with his policy of promoting sentiment above reality, and emotion above reason. To the Marquis

de Mirabeau, Rousseau admitted, 'all the harm that I have done in my life, I did as a result of reflection; what little good I have been able to do, I have done by impulse.'

Rousseau's aim was to make people, the people, happier by returning to nature. His recipe for achieving this was to invite people to copy him as a model. Unrivalled eloquence, artistry, simple religiosity and impassioned sincerity were his tools for spreading his gospel. Their effectiveness was all the greater because he introduced a revolution in literature. He contrived to make his readers, in a sense, his accomplices, even if they disagreed with him. The genre that he started has had the result of making poets and novelists more effective than priests or parsons, in bringing men face to face with their own consciences.

Rousseau's ideas seem to defy the passage of time. Nearly all the arguments advanced by him to prove that arts and sciences, social evolution and civilization have led to mankind's misery, were false. Nevertheless, if the question be asked today whether science and technology are continuing to improve the lot of mankind, what is the answer?

It is not generally known that Rousseau was the first Luddite. 'In everything relating to human industry, it is essential to forbid the use of any machine or invention which would shorten the time taken by the work, decrease the number of men working, or produce the same effect with less trouble.' There is a modern ring about those words. As for the spread of towns and factories at the expense of the countryside, industrial and social unrest, they echo Rousseau's warnings. Conservation of nature, the reaction against pollution, and desertion of town life in favour of the country, are the legitimate heirs to Rousseau's ideas.

The monument to Rousseau on the island that bears his name, in the middle of the Rhône where it flows out of the Lake of Geneva

CHRONOLOGY

1712 28 June: Rousseau born in Geneva
7 July: mother dies

1722 11 October: his father leaves Geneva for Nyon

1728 14 March: locked out of the Gates, Rousseau leaves Geneva
21 March: meets Mme de Warens at Annecy
21 April: he abjures Calvinism
Footman of Mme de Vercellis and of Comte de Gouvon

1729 June: Rousseau returns to Mme de Warens at Annecy

1730 Travels: Fribourg, Lausanne, Vevey, Neuchâtel

1731 June: first visit to Paris, and return to Annecy

1733 Mme de Warens becomes Rousseau's mistress

1736 Madame de Warens and Rousseau at Les Charmettes, Chambéry

1737 September: Rousseau goes to Montpellier; Mme de Larnage

1740 April: Rousseau accepts position as tutor to the sons of M. de Mably, at Lyons

1742 22 August: Rousseau presents his system of musical notation to the Académie royale des sciences in Paris

1743 Rousseau meets Mme Dupin and is appointed secretary to the French ambassador in Venice

1744 Rousseau is dismissed by the ambassador and returns via the Borromean Islands to Paris

1745 Rousseau becomes attached to Thérèse Levasseur

1746 His first child is abandoned to a foundling hospital

1749 October: on the way to see Diderot at Vincennes, Rousseau reads of the Dijon Academy competition and has a 'revelation'

1750 9 July. Rousseau's first *Discours* wins the prize at Dijon

1751 Rousseau's 'reform' first stage; he resigns from his secretaryship with Mme Dupin and copies music to live

1752 18 October: his *Le Devin du village* performed before the King at Fontainebleau; Rousseau refuses an audience

1754 1 August: Rousseau abjures Catholicism and resumes his rights as a citizen of Geneva

1755 April: Rousseau's second *Discours* (on inequality) is printed

1756 April: Rousseau's 'reform' second stage; he leaves Paris and lives

at L'Hermitage de Montmorency, placed at his disposal by Mme d'Épinay

1757 Rousseau's passion for Mme d'Houdetot, his rupture with Mme d'Épinay, and move to Mont-Louis, Montmorency

1758 *Lettre à d'Alembert sur les spectacles* published

1761 January: *La nouvelle Héloïse* published

1762 April: *Du Contrat social* published
May: *Émile* published
9 June: Paris issues warrant of arrest of Rousseau for *Émile*. He escapes to Yverdon in Switzerland
19 June: Geneva issues warrant of arrest for *Émile* and the *Contrat social*
10 July: expelled from Yverdon by the government of Berne, he crosses the Jura to Môtiers-Travers and lives in a house belonging to Mme Boy de la Tour

1763 March: *Lettre à Christophe de Beaumont* published
12 May: Rousseau renounces his citizenship of Geneva

1764 September: Rousseau is invited to draft a constitution for Corsica
December: *Lettres écrites de la montagne* published

1765 6 September: stones thrown at Rousseau's house at Môtiers-Travers

12 September: he takes refuge on the Île Saint-Pierre
25 October: he is expelled from the Île Saint-Pierre by the government of Berne and goes to Bienne
29 October: Rousseau leaves Bienne and Switzerland
16 December: Rousseau arrives in Paris

1766 4 January: Rousseau and David Hume leave Paris for London
13 January: arrival in London
31 January: Rousseau leaves for Chiswick
March: Rousseau inspects some houses in Surrey
22 March: Rousseau and Thérèse reach Wootton Hall, Staffs, and live in Richard Davenport's house
10 July: Rousseau writes his inimical letter to Hume

October: Hume publishes a *Concise Account of the Dispute*

1767 18 March: Rousseau receives a pension of £100 from George III
1 May: Rousseau and Thérèse leave Wootton Hall for Spalding
21 May: they embark at Dover for Calais
5 June: the Prince de Conti places Trye-le-Château at his disposal as a shelter; he calls himself Jean-Joseph Renou
November: Rousseau's *Dictionnaire de musique* printed

1768 10 June: Rousseau leaves Trye-le-Château for Lyons and Grenoble
30 August: Rousseau 'marries' Thérèse at Bourgoin

1770 June: Rousseau returns to Paris under his own name

1771 Rousseau finishes his *Confessions* and gives readings from them until forbidden by M. de Sartine, Lieutenant de Police

1772 Rousseau starts writing his *Dialogues*

1776 Rousseau starts writing his *Rêveries du promeneur solitaire*

1778 20 May: Rousseau accepts hospitality of the Marquis de Girardin at Ermenonville
2 July: death of Rousseau
4 July: his burial on the Île des Peupliers

1794 11 October: Rousseau's remains interred in the Panthéon, Paris

SELECT BIBLIOGRAPHY

Rousseau, Jean-Jacques, *Oeuvres complètes de Jean-Jacques Rousseau*, edited by B. Gagnebin and M. Raymond. Paris, Gallimard, Bibliothèque de la Pléiade, 4 vols., 1959–69. (A magnificent work of scholarship.)

Correspondance générale de Jean-Jacques Rousseau, edited by P.-P. Plan. Paris, Armand Colin, 20 vols., 1924–34. (Unreliable, incomplete; a new edition is in preparation by the Institut et Musée Voltaire, Geneva, edited by R. A. Leigh.)

Table à la Correspondance générale. Geneva, Droz, 1957.

Broome, J. H., *Jean-Jacques Rousseau in Staffordshire*. Keele University Library, Occasional Publication No. 1, 1966.

Burgelin, Pierre, *Jean-Jacques Rousseau et la religion de Génève*. Geneva, Labor et Fides, 1962.

Collins, J. Churton, *Voltaire, Montesquieu and Rousseau in England*. London, Eveleigh Nash, 1908.

Courtois, Louis-J., *Le Séjour de Jean-Jacques Rousseau en Angleterre*. Geneva, Jullien, 1911. (Many inaccurate identifications.)

Chronologie critique de la vie et des œuvres de Jean-Jacques Rousseau. Geneva, Jullien, 1924. (An invaluable work.)

de Beer, Gavin, 'Rousseau Botanist', *Annals of Science*. London, vol. 10, 1954.

'Quelques considerations sur le séjour de Jean-Jacques Rousseau en Angleterre', *Genava*. Geneva, vol. 3, 1955.

'Rousseau et les Anglais en Suisse', *Annales de la société Jean-Jacques Rousseau*. Geneva, vol. 33, 1955.

'Hominisation, humanisation, civilisation: réponse à Jean-Jacques Rousseau', *Archéocivilisation*. Paris, Picard, January–April 1966.

'Six lettres inédites de Jean-Jacques Rousseau', *Bulletin de la société d'histoire et d'archéologie de Génève*, vol. 13, 1966.

Ellis, H. Havelock, *From Rousseau to Proust*. London, Constable, 1936.

Gagnebin, Bernard, *A la recherche de Jean-Jacques Rousseau*. Geneva, Georg, 1962.

Guéhenno, Jean, *Jean-Jacques Rousseau*. London, Routledge, and New York, Colombia U.P., 1966.

Hilberer, J. E., 'Monsieur de Vautravers du Rockhall', *Annales de la société jurassienne d'émulation, année 1926*. Bienne, Gassmann, vol. 31, 1927. (Thomas Hollis's letter about Rousseau, p. 219.)

Jouvenel, Bertrand de, 'Jean-Jacques Rousseau', *Encounter*. London, 1962.

Leuba, Jean-Louis, 'Rousseau et l'orthodoxie éclairée', *Mélanges Rousseau*. Neuchâtel, Musée Neuchâtelois, 1962.

Lewin, Boleslao, *Rousseau y la independencia argentina y americana*. Buenos Aires, Eudeba, 1969.

May, Georges, *Rousseau par lui-même*. Paris, Seuil, 1961.

Ritter, Eugène, 'La famille et la jeunesse de Jean-Jacques Rousseau', *Annales de la société Jean-Jacques Rousseau*. Geneva, vol. 16, 1925.

Roddier, Henri, *Jean-Jacques Rousseau en Angleterre au XVIIIᵉ*. Paris, Boivin, 1950.

Spurlin, Paul Merrill, *Rousseau in America, 1760–1809*. Alabama U.P., 1969.

Voisine, Jacques, *Jean-Jacques Rousseau en Angleterre à l'époque romantique*. Paris, Didier, 1956.

NOTES ON THE PICTURES

Frontispiece: Jean-Jacques Rousseau; pastel on grey paper by Maurice-Quentin de La Tour, *c.* 1755. Musée d'Art et d'Histoire, Geneva (gift of Dr J.-Ch. Coindet).

5 The letter 'J' from a Republican alphabet decorated with engravings by Chemin the Younger, Paris An II. Bibliothèque Nationale, Paris.

6 View of Geneva from the lake; engraving from *Tableaux de la Suisse ou Voyage Pittoresque de la Suisse* by Laborde and Zurlauben, 1784 (2nd edition). British Museum. Photo R. B. Fleming.

8 Isaac Rousseau (1672-1747); early 18th-century ivory miniature. Bibliothèque Publique et Universitaire, Geneva. Photo B. Hermanjeat.

9 40, Grand' Rue, Geneva: the house where Jean-Jacques Rousseau was born in 1712. Photo André Halter.

10 Bossey, near Geneva; oil painting by Jacques Laurent Agasse, early 19th century. Musée Rousseau, Geneva. Photo Albert Grivel.

11 The Art of Etching and Engraving: engraving from Diderot's *Encyclopédie*, 1751-72. Mansell Collection, London.

Fortifications and drawbridge of Geneva; early 19th-century engraving, published by Monty. Bibliothèque Publique et Universitaire, Geneva. Photo B. Hermanjeat.

12 Madame de Warens (1699-1769); anonymous oil painting, *c.* 1730. Musée Rousseau, Geneva. Photo B. Hermanjeat.

13 Saint-François, Annecy (now the Cathédrale de Saint-Pierre). Photo copyright Société des Amis du Vieil Annecy.

14 View of the Piazza del Duomo, Turin, showing, at the back of the square, the Via Porta Palatino, in which the Ospizio dello Spirito Santo was situated. Engraving by Friedrich Bernhard Werner, *c.* 1730. Biblioteca Nazionale Universitaria de Torino.

16 Jean-Jacques Rousseau guiding the horses of Mlle de Graffenried and Mlle Galley across the stream; lithograph by Solange Tessier, Bibliothèque Publique et Universitaire, Geneva. Photo B. Hermanjeat.

The Cherry Pickers; gouache on paper by Pierre Antoine Baudoin, *c.* 1765. Private collection.

17 View of Lausanne; coloured engraving of the second half of the 18th century by J. L. Alberli and B. A. Dunker. Musée du Vieux Lausanne. Photo copyright Bibliothèque Cantonale et Universitaire, Lausanne.

Plaque on what is now the Café de la Clef, Vevey, where Jean-Jacques Rousseau stayed in 1730. Photo Swiss National Tourist Office.

18 View of Fribourg; engraving from *Les États et les Délices de la Suisse*, vol. II by Ruchat, 1764. British Museum. Photo R. B. Fleming.

19 *The Wretched Poor*, pen, ink and watercolour on paper by Louis Watteau de Lille, 1795. Private Collection.

Jean-Jacques Rousseau at Les Charmettes; 18th-century engraving by Gossard. Bibliothèque Nationale, Paris. Photo Bulloz.

21 Letter from Isaac Rousseau to Mme de Warens, dated 22nd August 1740, referring to his son's employment as tutor to the two sons of Monsieur de Mably. Bibliothèque Publique et Universitaire, Geneva. Photo Jean Arlaud.

22 Example of Jean-Jacques Rousseau's system of musical notation. Bibliothèque Publique et Universitaire, Geneva. Photo B. Hermanjeat.

23 Mme Louise-Marie-Madeleine Dupin (1707-99); oil painting by Jean Marc Nattier, *c.* 1760-65. Collection Mrs A. Tyrer, Rilly-sur-Vienne. Photo Arsicaud, Tours.

24 Jean-Jacques Rousseau as secretary to the Ambassador of France in Venice; anonymous oil painting, *c.* 1743. Bibliothèque Publique et Universitaire, Geneva. Photo Albert Grivel.

25 Entrance to the Canareggio, Venice; oil painting by a Guardi imitator, not earlier than 1804. By courtesy of the Trustees of the National Gallery, London.

26 Courtyard in Venice; oil painting by Francesco Guardi. By permission of the Trustees of the Wallace Collection, London.

27 The Grand Canal, Venice; oil painting from the studio of Canaletto, after 1753. By permission of the Trustees of the Wallace Collection, London.

28 The Yew Tree Ball given at Versailles at the time of the marriage of the Dauphin in 1745. Rousseau was commissioned to alter a ballet by Voltaire and Rameau written in honour of this same occasion.. Engraving by Cochin the Younger, *c.* 1745. Louvre, Paris. Photo Bulloz.

29 Jean-Jacques Rousseau's house in the rue Plâtrière, Paris; engraving by C. de Last after Lameau from *Vues de différentes habitations de Jean-Jacques Rousseau*, 1819. British Museum. Photo R.B. Fleming.

Sisters of St Vincent de Paul caring for the foundlings of Paris. Early 19th-century lithograph by Marlet. By courtesy of the Wellcome Trustees.

30 Frontispiece to Diderot's *Encyclopédie*; engraved by Claude Nicolas Cochin the Younger, 1751. British Museum. Photo R.B. Fleming.

Title-page of the first volume of Diderot's *Encyclopédie*, 1751. British Museum. Photo R.B. Fleming.

31 Denis Diderot (1713–84); oil painting by L.M. Van Loo, 1767. Louvre, Paris. Photo Giraudon.

Donjon of the Castle at Vincennes, built *c.* 1360.

33 Woman of high standing soliciting a judge; early 18th-century engraving by N. Arnoult. British Museum.

Dusky Bay, New Zealand; oil painting by William Hodges, R.A., 1777. The Lords Commissioners of the Admiralty. Photo Royal Academy of Arts, London.

34 Specimen of music copied by Jean-Jacques Rousseau (MS fr 233); Bibliothèque Publique et Universitaire, Geneva. Photo B. Hermanjeat.

35 Title-page of Jean-Jacques Rousseau's opera *Le Devin du village*, 1753. Bibliothèque Publique et Universitaire, Geneva. Photo Jean Arlaud.

Illustration from *Le Devin du village*, first published in 1753; engraving of the last quarter of the 18th century by Moreau le Jeune. Bibliothèque Nationale, Paris. Photo Bulloz.

36 Illustration from *Narcisse*, an opera by Jean-Jacques Rousseau first published in 1753; engraving of the last quarter of the 18th century after N. Monsiaux. Bibliothèque Publique et Universitaire, Geneva. Photo Jean Arlaud.

37 Title-page to *Discours sur l'origine et les fondemens de l'inégalité parmi les hommes* by Jean-Jacques Rousseau, published Amsterdam 1755. British Museum. Photo R.B. Fleming.

38 Louis Georges Leclerc, Comte de Buffon (1707–88); late 18th-century allegorical engraving after C.P. Marillier. British Museum.

42 View on the Lake of Geneva; engraving of the second half of the 18th century after J. Sybrast. British Museum.

43 Voltaire (François-Marie Arouet) (1694–1778); oil painting by Théodore Gardelle, *c.* 1745–50. British Museum.

Les coups de pied, illustration from *Candide* by Voltaire, Berlin edition, 1785; engraving. British Museum. Photo R.B. Fleming.

44 Madame d'Épinay; pastel on paper by Jean-Étienne Liotard, *c.* 1759. Musée d'Art et d'Histoire, Geneva. (Gift of Monsieur Tronchin-Bertrand.)

Hermitage at Montmorency; 18th-century engraving by Gossard. Bibliothèque Publique et Universitaire, Geneva. Photo B. Hermanjeat.

45 *Le premier baiser d'amour*, illustration from *Julie, ou La nouvelle Héloïse* by Jean-Jacques Rousseau, Amsterdam edition, 1764; engraving after H. Gravelot by N. Le Mire, 1760. British Museum. Photo R.B. Fleming.

L'Amour maternel, illustration from *Julie, ou La nouvelle Héloïse* by Jean-Jacques Rousseau, Amsterdam edition, 1764; engraving after H. Gravelot by Longueil. British Museum. Photo R.B. Fleming.

46 *Les monumens des anciennes amours*, illustration from *Julie, ou La nouvelle Héloïse*, edition of 1774(?); engraving after H. Gravelot by P. Choffard. British Museum. Photo John Freeman.

47 Forest of Montmorency (the chestnut tree associated with Jean-Jacques Rousseau, in the foreground). Photo Plotard.

48 View of the Borromean Islands on Lake Maggiore; coloured lithograph by G. Berettini, no. 2 of *Views of Lake Maggiore and Lake Como*, published Milan, 1810. Map Room, British Museum. Photo R.B. Fleming.

Crusoe saving his goods out of the wreck of the ship, illustration from *Robinson Crusoe* by Daniel Defoe, London edition, 1726; engraving. British Museum. Photo R.B. Fleming.

49 View of Clarens on the Lake of Geneva; engraving by F.G. Wexelberg, *c.* 1770–80. Bibliothèque Cantonale et Universitaire, Lausanne.

50 Draft of a letter from Jean-Jacques Rousseau to Madame d'Houdetot, 1757. Bibliothèque Publique et Universitaire, Geneva.

51 Summer-house at Mont-Louis, Montmorency (Val-d'Oise). Photo Plotard.

Mont-Louis, Montmorency (Val-d'Oise). Photo Plotard.

52 Jean-le-Rond d'Alembert (1717–83); Pastel on paper by Maurice-Quentin de La Tour, 1753. Louvre, Paris. Photo Archives Photographiques.

Title-page of *A Monsieur d'Alembert* by Jean-Jacques Rousseau, published Amsterdam, 1758. British Museum. Photo R.B. Fleming.

54 Title-page of *Lettres de deux Amants* (*Julie, ou La nouvelle Héloïse*) by Jean-Jacques Rousseau, published Amsterdam, 1761. British Museum. Photo R.B. Fleming.

Illustration from *Clarissa* by Samuel Richardson; engraving from French edition of 1777. British Museum.

55 Illustration for *Julie, ou La nouvelle Héloïse* by Jean-Jacques Rousseau; ink and wash drawing by Francis Wheatley, 1786. Prints and Drawings, British Museum.

56 Title-page of the *Contrat social* by Jean-Jacques Rousseau, published Amsterdam, 1762. British Museum. Photo John Freeman.

Jean-Jacques Rousseau holding a copy of his *Contrat social*; anonymous 18th-century oil painting. Collection of Sir Walter and Lady Bromley Davenport. Photo Entwhistle, Thorpe and Co. Ltd., Manchester.

57 *A Democrat*; cartoon by De Vinck, 1757, published London, 1791, by J.W. Fores of Piccadilly. Bibliothèque Nationale, Paris.

The Fête of the Supreme Being; engraving *c.* 1796. Bibliothèque Nationale, Paris. Photo Françoise Foliot.

58 Jean-Jacques Rousseau composing *Émile* in the valley of Montmorency; mid-18th-century engraving after Albrier. Bibliothèque Nationale, Paris. Photo Giraudon.

59 Frontispiece to *Émile, ou de L'Éducation* by Jean-Jacques Rousseau, showing Thetis and her son, Achilles; engraving from edition of 1793. British Museum.

Title-page to *Émile, ou de L'Éducation* by Jean-Jacques Rousseau, published Amsterdam, 1762. British Museum. Photo R.B. Fleming.

60 'Souvenez-vous que j'irai labourer vos sèves si vous touchez à mes melons', illustration from *Émile, ou de L'Éducation* by Jean-Jacques Rousseau; engraving after C.P. Marillier from French edition of 1785 (?) British Museum. Photo R.B. Fleming.

'De sa blanche et débile main, elle poussa un rabot sur la planche', illustration from *Émile, ou de L'Éducation* by Jean-Jacques Rousseau; engraving from the French edition of 1785 (?) British Museum. Photo R.B. Fleming.

61 Duc de Luxembourg, Marshal of France (1702–64); engraving, 1793. Mansell Collection, London.

63 Warrant issued by the Parlement on 9 June 1761 for the burning of *Émile*. Archives de France, Paris. Photo La Société Française du Microfilm, Paris.

View of the town of Yverdon showing the Faubourg de la Plaine, where Daniel Roguin lived in 1762; detail of an engraving by D. Hershberger, 1756. Bibliothèque Cantonale et Universitaire, Lausanne.

64 The river Doubs near Neuchâtel, the area of Jean-Jacques Rousseau's botanical excursions in 1762. Photo Swiss National Tourist Office.

65 View of the village of Môtiers-Travers with the house of Jean-Jacques Rousseau; engraving from *Tableaux de la Suisse, ou Voyage Pittoresque de la Suisse* by Laborde and Zurlauben, 1784. British Museum. Photo R.B. Fleming.

Waterfall of the river Doubs in the area of Jean-Jacques Rousseau's botanical excursions in 1762. Photo French Government Tourist Office.

66 Christophe de Beaumont, Archbishop of Paris; engraving by R. Gaillard after J. Chevallier, *c.* 1762. Bibliothèque Nationale, Paris.

67 'Je crois donc que le monde est gouverné par une volonté puisante et sage', illustration from *Émile, ou de L'Éducation* by Jean-Jacques Rousseau; engraving after C.P. Marillier from French edition of 1785 (?) British Museum. Photo R.B. Fleming.

Title-page of *A Christophe de Beaumont* by Jean-Jacques Rousseau, published Amsterdam, 1763. British Museum. Photo R.B. Fleming.

68 Detail of title-page of *Lettres écrites de la montagne* by Jean-Jacques Rousseau, showing the author's motto, *vitam impendere vero*; published Amsterdam, 1764. British Museum. Photo R.B. Fleming.

69 Voltaire and Jean-Jacques Rousseau quarrelling; engraving *c.* 1760-70. Bibliothèque Nationale, Paris.

71 View of the Île Saint-Pierre from the shores of the Lake of Bienne; engraving by Johann Joseph Hartmann, 1807. Bibliothèque Nationale Suisse, Berne.

72 View of the Île Saint-Pierre on the Lake of Bienne, showing the house where Jean-Jacques Rousseau stayed in September 1765. Photo Swiss National Tourist Office.

Living room of the house on the Île Saint-Pierre in which Jean-Jacques Rousseau stayed in September 1765. Photo Swiss National Tourist Office.

73 *L'Embarquement des Lapins*, illustration from *Les Confessions* by Jean-Jacques Rousseau, showing Rousseau, Thérèse, his dog Sultan, with the Receiver's wife and sister, taking rabbits to inhabit a tiny island south of the Île Saint-Pierre on the Lake of Bienne; late 18th-century engraving by N. Monsiaux. Bibliothèque Nationale, Paris.

Bedroom which Jean-Jacques Rousseau used during his stay on the Île Saint-Pierre in September 1765; engraving from *Vues de différentes habitations de Jean-Jacques Rousseau*, 1819. British Museum. Photo R.B. Fleming.

74 Rockhall, the house at Bienne belonging to Rodolphe Vautravers where Jean-Jacques Rousseau stayed in October 1765; pen drawing by Johann Joseph Hartmann, *c.* 1800-10. Musée Schwab, Bienne.

William Kenrick at thirty-six years (1725-1779); engraving by T. Worlidge, *c.* 1765. National Portrait Gallery, London.

75 Paul Moultou, pastor of Geneva (1725-85); anonymous oil painting of the third quarter of the 18th century. Bibliothèque Publique et Universitaire, Geneva. Photo B. Hermanjeat.

Thomas Hollis (1720-74); engraving, 1788. Mansell Collection, London.

James Boswell (1740-95) in the dress of an armed Corsican chief as he appeared at Shakespeare's Jubilee at Stratford-upon-Avon in September 1769; engraving by J. Miller, *c.* 1770. National Portrait Gallery, London.

76 Dr John Turton, F.R.S., later physician to George III; oil painting by Francis Cotes, *c.* 1758-65. Collection R.H. Turton, M.P., Upsall Castle. Photo Hodgson, Northallerton.

View of the castle and town of Dover; engraving by J. Mason after G. Lambert, 1762. Map Room British Museum. Photo R.B. Fleming.

77 No. 10 Buckingham Street, off the Strand, London, where Jean-Jacques Rousseau stayed in 1766. Photo Greater London Council.

78 David Hume (1711-76); oil painting by Allan Ramsay, 1766. National Gallery of Scotland, Edinburgh. Photo Annan, Glasgow.

View of Monaughty in Radnorshire, the house which Jean-Jacques Rousseau was offered in 1766, but refused. Photo C.V. Hancock, Birmingham.

79 David Garrick and Miss Younge in the characters of Lusignan and Zara, in *Zara*. An earlier performance of 1766 was seen by Jean-Jacques Rousseau in which Garrick also played Lusignan. Engraving by Collyer, 1777. Prints and Drawings, Victoria and Albert Museum, London. Photo Eileen Tweedy.

View of Chiswick, in Middlesex; mid-18th-century engraving. Mansell Collection, London.

80 James Boswell (1740-95); late 18th-century engraving by F. Holl from a sketch by Sir Thomas Lawrence, P.R.A. Mansell Collection, London.

Horace Walpole, 4th Earl of Orford (1717-97); oil painting by J.G. Eccardt, 1754. National Portrait Gallery, London.

81 Detail of a map of Surrey engraved by Peter Andrews after John Rocque, 1768. Map Room, British Museum.

Mundies Farm, Wotton, Surrey, where Jean-Jacques Rousseau stayed in 1766. Photo J.T. May, Guildford.

82 The Rookery, near Dorking, where Daniel Malthus was living in 1766; drawing by J. Gendell after an engraving by R. Ackerman, 1823. Sir Gavin de Beer, F.R.S., F.S.A.

83 Wotton Place, Surrey, where Sir John Evelyn was living in 1766; after an engraving by J. Basire, mid-18th century. Photo Department of the Environment.

Statue erected to Jean-Jacques Rousseau in the park at Wotton Place, Surrey, by W.J. Evelyn, c. 1880. Photo J.T. May, Guildford.

84 Wootton Hall, Staffordshire; the house which Richard Davenport placed at the disposal of Jean-Jacques Rousseau from the end of March, 1766. Photo in the possession of Sir Walter and Lady Bromley Davenport.

Richard Davenport (1705-71); anonymous oil painting, c. 1750-

60. Collection D.W.H. Neilson, Esq. Photo Paul Mellon Centre for Studies of British Art (London) Ltd.

85 General Henry Seymour Conway, Secretary of State (1721-95); wax medallion by J. Gosscett, 1760. National Portrait Gallery, London.

George III; polychrome statuette by F. Hardenberg, 1820. National Portrait Gallery, London.

86 Anne-Robert-Jacques Turgot, Baron de l'Aulne; contemporary oil painting by Joseph Ducreux, undated. Musée de Versailles. Photo Réunion des Musées Nationaux.

87 Title-page of *A Concise and Genuine Account of the Dispute between Mr Hume and Mr Rousseau* by David Hume, published London, 1766. British Museum. Photo R.B. Fleming.

89 View in Dovedale, Derbyshire; watercolour by Joseph Wright of Derby, 1780-85. Derby Art Gallery. Photo Courtauld Institute of Art, London.

90 *L'homme de la Nature*: Jean-Jacques Rousseau botanizing; coloured lithograph by C. de Last after Mayer, from *Vues de différentes habitations de Jean-Jacques Rousseau*, 1819. British Museum. Photo R.B. Fleming.

View near Carleton, Derbyshire; engraving by E. Francis after W. Westall, c. 1830-50. Mansell Collection, London.

91 Erasmus Darwin, grandfather of Charles Darwin the biologist (1731-1802); oil painting by

Joseph Wright of Derby, c. 1785. Down House. Photo copyright Royal College of Surgeons, London.

92 View of Spalding market-place with the White Hart Inn where Jean-Jacques Rousseau arrived on 5 May 1766; engraving by H. Burgess, 1822. Map Room, British Museum. Photo R.B. Fleming.

93 Charles Pratt, Lord Camden, Lord High Chancellor (1714-94); oil painting by Nathaniel Dance, undated. National Portrait Gallery London.

94 Jean-Jacques Rousseau; the original oil painting by Allan Ramsay, 1766. National Gallery of Scotland, Edinburgh. Photo Annan, Glasgow.

95 Jean-Jacques Rousseau; copy (oil on canvas) of the 1766 Ramsay portrait, by the same artist for Richard Davenport, 1767. Collection Sir Walter and Lady Bromley-Davenport. Photo Entwhistle, Thorpe and Co. Ltd., Manchester.

96 Nuneham Courtenay, the seat of the 2nd Earl Harcourt, a great admirer of Jean-Jacques Rousseau; watercolour by Paul Sandby, c. 1782. Oxford University Chest Estates. Photo Mavis Batey.

97 View of the Hôtel-dieu and the Chaussée St Leu at Amiens; lithograph from *Views of Amiens* by E. Balan, 1835-45. Prints and Drawings, British Museum. Photo R.B. Fleming.

Notre-Dame, Abbeville; lithograph of 1821 from a drawing by J. Fudge, 1820. Prints and Drawings, British Museum. Photo R.B. Fleming.

INDEX

References in italics are to page numbers on
which captions appear